Good Housekeeping's
CASSEROLE COOKERY

By the
Food Editors
of
Good
Housekeeping
Magazine

ILLUSTRATIONS BY
KINUKO CRAFT

PHOTOGRAPHS BY
JAMES VILES

Published by
Consolidated Book Publishers
1727 South Indiana Avenue, Chicago, Illinois 60616

Contents

What's the most convenient, time-saving, and *flavorful* word in cooking today? Casseroles, of course. And just look what they have in their *flavor*: Many casseroles may be fully prepared yesterday, or early today, and forgotten. All they'll need is a little warming time before dinner time. *Casserole Cookery* As for what goes into them, there's something miraculous that happens when contrasting tastes get to know each other. (This brings to mind the heavenly aromas that seem to surround casseroles . . . mmmmmm!) § Any time of year is the right season for casseroles. For instance, any one of the three at the right might fill the bill on a warm summer night or a cold winter day. The Baked Alaska Meat Loaf is an entirely new idea; it's baked right in the mixing bowl. The Fish with a Bouquet of Vegetables can make those usually boring Lenten meals a real pleasure. Or try Savory Filled Eggs and Asparagus. § What else? More and more main dishes, exciting vegetable minglings, and breads *en casserole*. Even desserts—just what your mouth has been set for—and many of them may be baked right along with the main dish. Ready? Start now.

Meat Casseroles

BAKED ALASKA MEAT LOAF
(Pictured on page 2)

3 eggs, unbeaten	1 cup grated raw carrots
4 teaspoons salt	½ cup snipped parsley
¼ teaspoon pepper	2 boxes (8-serving size)
3 cups fresh white-bread	instant fluffy mashed
crumbs	potatoes
½ cup chili sauce	3 egg yolks, unbeaten
½ cup minced onion	1 tablespoon prepared
4 pounds lean chuck,	mustard
ground	

Early on day:
1. In large bowl beat eggs; stir in salt, pepper, bread crumbs, chili sauce, and onion; lightly mix in chuck, carrots, and parsley.
2. Pack meat mixture into 2-quart ovenproof mixing bowl; cover with saran and refrigerate.
About 3 hours before serving:
1. Start heating oven to 400°F.
2. Bake meat loaf 1 hour and 30 to 40 minutes, draining off fat during baking.
3. Invert meat loaf on wire rack to drain; then slide onto wooden plank or greased cookie sheet; pat dry with paper towel.
4. Meanwhile, prepare 1 box potatoes as package label directs, using 3½ cups total liquid. Repeat with second box. In large bowl, combine potatoes; beat in egg yolks with mustard. Use to thickly frost loaf as pictured.
5. Then, in same oven, bake about 30 minutes, or until golden. Makes 8 to 10 servings.

MEAL-IN-ONE BEEF CASSEROLE

2 tablespoons shortening	1 8-ounce can whole-kernel
1 medium onion, chopped	corn, drained
1½ pounds chuck, ground	1 10-ounce package frozen
1½ teaspoons salt	mixed vegetables,
⅛ teaspoon pepper	cooked, drained
½ teaspoon dill seeds	1 cup commercial sour
1 envelope mushroom-soup	cream
mix	2 cups packaged bite-size
	rice cereal

Early on day:
1. In skillet, in hot shortening, sauté onion and chuck until lightly browned, stirring occasionally with a fork.
2. Add salt, pepper, dill seeds, and mushroom-soup mix. Stir in 1 cup hot water until well blended, then

corn, mixed vegetables, and sour cream. Spoon mixture into 12-by-8-by-2-inch baking dish. Cover; refrigerate.
About 35 minutes before serving:
1. Start heating oven to 350°F.
2. Uncover casserole; sprinkle rice cereal evenly over top.
3. Bake 30 minutes, or until hot, covering loosely with foil after 15 minutes to prevent overbrowning of cereal.
4. Serve hot. Nice with herb-buttered French bread, potato salad in lettuce cups, and grapes in lime gelatin. Makes 6 servings.
Note: Casserole may be made, then baked immediately after preparation for 15 to 20 minutes.

HAMBURGER CRUNCH

2 tablespoons shortening	1 soup-can water
½ pound chuck, ground	¼ cup uncooked regular
once	white rice
1 small onion, chopped	2 tablespoons soy sauce
½ 10½-ounce can con-	Speck pepper
densed chicken soup,	½ 3-ounce can chow-mein
undiluted	noodles
½ 10½-ounce can con-	
densed cream-of-mush-	
room soup, undiluted	

About 1 hour and 10 minutes before serving:
1. Start heating oven to 350°F.
2. In skillet, in hot shortening, sauté chuck until it loses its red color; add onion, cook 5 minutes.
3. In greased 1½-quart casserole combine hamburger mixture with soups, water, rice, soy sauce, and pepper.
4. Bake, uncovered, 50 minutes. Sprinkle chow-mein noodles over hamburger; bake 10 minutes longer.
5. Remove from oven; let stand 10 minutes before serving. Makes 3 servings.
FOR 6: Double all ingredients; prepare and bake as directed above.

DUTCH HASH

¼ cup butter or margarine	2 cups crushed pretzels
2 large green peppers,	¼ cup snipped parsley
cut in large chunks	1 teaspoon dill seeds
2 large onions, sliced	½ teaspoon seasoned
1 pound chuck, ground	pepper
1 1-pound 3-ounce can	½ teaspoon dry mustard
tomatoes	½ to ¾ teaspoon salt

About 1 hour and 30 minutes before serving:
1. Start heating oven to 350°F.
2. In large skillet, or Dutch oven, over low heat, melt butter. Add green peppers, and onions; sauté just until fork-tender.
3. Stir in chuck; cook until meat just loses its red color. Remove one third of mixture. Into meat left in

skillet stir tomatoes, pretzels, parsley, dill seeds, pepper, mustard, and salt. Turn mixture into 2½-quart casserole. Top with reserved third of meat mixture.
4. Bake, covered with lid or foil, about 30 minutes, or until hot.
5. Serve with chilled asparagus with Hollandaise, thawed frozen croissants, and fruited gelatin parfaits. Makes 4 to 6 servings.

BEEF 'N' BEAN BAKE

3 slices bacon	1 1-pound can lima beans,
1 large onion, sliced	drained
1 pound chuck, ground	2 tablespoons brown sugar
1 10½-ounce can con-	1½ teaspoons salt
densed tomato soup,	¼ teaspoon pepper
undiluted	

About 50 minutes before serving:
1. Start heating oven to 350°F.
2. In large skillet, sauté bacon until nearly crisp; remove bacon. In bacon fat left in skillet, sauté onion until golden; add chuck and sauté, stirring occasionally, to desired rareness. Remove from heat; stir in soup, beans, brown sugar, salt, and pepper. Transfer mixture to 1½-quart casserole. Lay bacon on top.
3. Bake 25 minutes, or until hot.
4. Serve with sour cream-topped baked potatoes, asparagus vinaigrette, and rhubarb sauce with spice-cake squares. Makes 3 or 4 servings.

HAMBURGER-BAKED BEAN CASSEROLE
(Pictured on page 6)

2 tablespoons butter or	4 1-pound cans Boston-
margarine	style baked beans
6 medium onions, thinly	2 pounds chuck, ground
sliced	¼ cup soy sauce
2 cups sliced celery tops	3 tablespoons liquid
2 dashes Tabasco	honey
1 teaspoon dried thyme	½ teaspoon salt
½ teaspoon salt	2 tablespoons butter or
¼ teaspoon pepper	margarine

About 1 hour and 30 minutes before serving:
1. Start heating oven to 350°F.
2. In skillet, in 2 tablespoons butter, sauté onions and celery tops 5 minutes; add Tabasco, thyme, ½ teaspoon salt, and pepper.
3. Meanwhile, heat beans; with 2-tined fork, stir in onion mixture.
4. With 2-tined fork, combine chuck, soy sauce, honey, and ½ teaspoon salt; shape into 1-inch balls. In 2 tablespoons butter, sauté one third of meat balls until browned.
5. Arrange one third of bean mixture in 3-quart casserole; top with sautéed meat balls. Sauté another third

of meat balls; use to top another layer of beans. Repeat once more.
6. Bake casserole, covered, 20 minutes.
7. Serve with hot coleslaw, a basket of blueberry muffins, and a bowl of pretzels as pictured, with Spanish cream and walnut cookies for dessert. Makes 12 to 16 servings.

FOR 3 OR 4: Use 1 onion, ¼ cup celery tops, 1 tablespoon butter or margarine, dash Tabasco, ¼ teaspoon dried thyme, ¼ teaspoon salt, speck pepper, 1 can baked beans, ½ pound ground chuck, 1 tablespoon soy sauce, 1 tablespoon honey, ¼ teaspoon salt, and 1 tablespoon butter or margarine. Make as above, but sauté all meat at once.

HIS CHILI

½ pound link sausage,	½ cup uncooked corn meal
sliced	1 12-ounce can whole-
1½ pounds chuck, ground	kernel corn
2 medium onions, chopped	1 small can pitted ripe
2 teaspoons salt	olives, drained
¼ teaspoon pepper	½ cup grated natural or
1 tablespoon chili powder	process Cheddar cheese
1 cup milk	(¼ pound)
2 8-ounce cans tomato	
sauce	

Early on day:
1. In large skillet, slowly brown sausage, pouring off fat as it accumulates; add chuck and onions; cook until chuck loses its red color. Add salt, pepper, chili powder, milk, and tomato sauce. Cover and simmer about 20 minutes.
2. Now, in 3-quart casserole, stir corn meal and corn together. Add chuck mixture and stir together; sprinkle olives and cheese on top. Refrigerate.
About 1 hour and 10 minutes before serving:
1. Start heating oven to 375°F.
2. Bake casserole 55 minutes, or until piping hot.
3. Serve with tossed salad, assorted crackers, fresh pineapple wedges, and chocolate cookies. Makes 6 to 8 servings.

Hamburger-Baked Bean Casserole

Quick Tamale Pie

MEAT-BALL STEW EN CASSEROLE

2 pounds potatoes, pared,
    quartered
1½ pounds small white
    onions
1 bunch small carrots,
    halved lengthwise
1 package frozen peas,
    thawed
2 pounds chuck, ground
1 egg, unbeaten
1 cup day-old bread
    crumbs
¾ teaspoon marjoram
2½ teaspoons salt

¾ teaspoon Worcestershire
⅔ cup milk
⅓ cup salad oil
1½ pounds small fresh
    mushrooms
1 10½-ounce can con-
    densed cream-of-mush-
    room soup, undiluted
¾ teaspoon nutmeg
¾ teaspoon bottled sauce
    for gravy
¾ teaspoon onion salt or
    monosodium glutamate

Early on day:

1.   In large saucepan place quartered potatoes in layer, then onions, then carrots. Cook in 1 inch boiling salted water, covered, 20 minutes, or until vegetables are barely tender-crisp; top with peas; cover; turn off heat.
2.   Meanwhile, with fork, lightly mix chuck with unbeaten egg, bread crumbs, marjoram, salt, Worcestershire, and milk. Into hot salad oil, in skillet, drop meat mixture by teaspoonfuls; brown quickly on all sides; remove.
3.   In same skillet, sauté mushrooms until tender; remove. Then, in skillet, heat soup with nutmeg, bottled sauce for gravy, and onion salt.
4.   In 3-quart casserole, arrange drained peas, carrots, onions, mushrooms, and meat balls. Near edge of casserole pour in sauce. Mash and season drained potatoes; arrange in mounds around top edge of casserole; refrigerate.

About 50 minutes before serving:

1.   Start heating oven to 400°F.
2.   Bake casserole, uncovered, 35 minutes, or until browned and bubbly. Makes 8 servings.

QUICK TAMALE PIE
(Pictured opposite)

1½ cups yellow corn meal
3 15½-ounce cans chili
    con carne with beans
2 16-ounce cans kidney
    beans, drained
½ cup instant minced
    onion (8 tablespoons)
1½ tablespoons paprika
    (4½ teaspoons)

½ teaspoon curry powder
Pitted ripe olives
Condiments: Light or dark
    raisins, sliced almonds,
    grated cheese, diced
    dill pickle, corn relish,
    grated orange peel

Day before, or early on day:

Use corn meal to make mush as package label directs. Pour into 3-quart casserole; cover with foil or wax paper, placed directly on mush; refrigerate.

About 1 hour before serving:

1.   Start heating oven to 400°F.
2.   In large saucepan heat chili con carne, kidney beans, onion, paprika, and curry powder until hot, stirring occasionally.
3.   When beans are hot, with back of spoon, press mush against sides of casserole to form a lining 1 inch thick. Spread rest of mush over bottom of casserole. Immediately fill with hot bean mixture.
4.   Bake casserole about 1 hour.
5.   Top with a ring of ripe olives; serve with condiments and assorted crackers as pictured. Makes 12 servings.

FOR 4: Use one half of corn meal, chili con carne, kidney beans, minced onion, paprika, and curry powder and 1½-quart casserole. Bake 30 minutes.

OVEN BEEF STEW

2 pounds boned chuck or
    bottom round, in 2-inch
    cubes
¼ cup regular all-purpose
    flour
3 tablespoons salad oil
1 teaspoon monosodium
    glutamate
1 teaspoon salt
3 tablespoons prepared
    mustard

2½ cups canned tomato
    juice or water
12 small white onions
12 small carrots,
    quartered lengthwise
1 10-ounce package frozen
    whole-kernel corn,
    thawed just enough to
    separate

1.   Start heating oven to 350°F.
2.   Sprinkle meat with flour. Reserve leftover flour.
3.   In hot oil, in skillet, brown meat cubes well on all sides — 15 to 20 minutes. Remove meat to 3-quart casserole.
4.   Into oil, stir monosodium glutamate, salt, mustard, and any remaining flour. Slowly add tomato juice, stirring constantly; then pour over meat.
5.   Bake, covered, 1 hour. Add onions and carrots. Bake, covered, 45 minutes. Add corn. Bake, covered, 15 minutes longer, or until meat and vegetables are tender.
6.   Before serving, stir stew with fork to bring meat chunks to top. Makes 6 servings.

TO VARY: Add 12 pared small potatoes with carrots; substitute peas for corn.

LAMB STEW: For beef, substitute 2 pounds boned lamb shoulder, with as much fat trimmed off as possible. Increase flour to 5 tablespoons. Before stirring stew to serve it, spoon off any fat that may have risen to surface during cooking.

VEAL STEW: Substitute 2 pounds boned veal shoulder for beef, 1 to 1½ cups white wine for 1 to 1½ cups of tomato juice, and ½ pound fresh mushrooms for corn. Use 5 tablespoons flour.

For a twosome, choose any of the variations pictured. Start heating oven to 375°F. Take 1 1-pound 4-ounce can of favorite brand beef stew; add the seasonings indicated. Place in 2 individual casseroles of at least 1½-cup capacity. Bake on sheet of foil; complete as directed.

Amandine: Season beef stew with 1 tablespoon instant minced onion, 1 tablespoon sherry, ⅛ teaspoon pepper, and, if desired, ¼ cup commercial sour cream. Top each casserole with 2 tablespoons slivered almonds, sprinkled in border around edge as pictured. Bake about 20 minutes, or until hot and bubbly.

Begin with Beef Stew

Potpie Paprika: Season beef stew with ½ teaspoon paprika. Unroll 1 can refrigerated crescent rolls; from it cut 2 circles, each ½ inch larger than top of casserole. Place on casseroles, fluting edges; brush with milk. Bake 25 minutes.

Muffin Topknot: Season beef stew with ½ teaspoon chili powder and 1 tablespoon instant minced onion. Bake in 2 casseroles 20 minutes. Then top each with a corn-muffin half, cut-side down; sprinkle with shredded process Cheddar cheese. Bake 3 to 5 minutes, or until cheese is melted.

New England Pinwheel: Season beef stew with 1 teaspoon prepared mustard and 1 teaspoon horse-radish. Bake in 2 casseroles 20 minutes. Remove dough from 1 can refrigerated crescent rolls; for each casserole, cut 3 to 5 slices, ½ inch thick; lay, cut-side up, on top of each casserole; brush with milk and bake 10 minutes.

Old-English Crisscross: Season beef stew with ¾ teaspoon Worcestershire. From piecrust-mix dough cut 2 circles as large as top of casseroles; then cut out centers, leaving 1-inch border of piecrust. For each also cut 4 strips of dough, about 5 inches by ¾ inch. Use strips to form lattice on each casserole; set piecrust border on top; brush with milk. Bake 30 to 35 minutes, or until crust is browned.

Creole Okra: Season beef stew with 1 tablespoon instant minced onion and ½ teaspoon gumbo filé or chili powder. Top each casserole with 3 frozen okra pods. Cover with foil; bake about 35 minutes.

BEGIN WITH BEEF STEW *(Continued)*

Mushroomed: Season beef stew with ¼ teaspoon caraway seeds and ⅛ teaspoon salt. Set 5 washed, small fresh mushrooms on top of each casserole, spoke-fashion, as pictured on page 8; brush with melted butter; sprinkle with salt. Bake 25 minutes. Tuck a bit of water cress upright in center of each.

Tomato Topper: Season beef stew with ½ teaspoon curry powder and speck pepper; bake in 2 casseroles 20 minutes. Then top each with 2 tomato slices, ½ inch thick, as pictured on page 8. Sprinkle with salt and seasoned pepper. Bake 10 minutes longer.

Continental Kidney Bean: Season beef stew with ½ teaspoon rosemary, 1 tablespoon red wine, and speck pepper. Top each casserole with ½ cup canned kidney beans, tossing them in lightly with fork. Cover with foil; bake 10 minutes; then uncover and bake 15 minutes longer.

> *What size casserole? Recipes usually call for casseroles in quart sizes. If yours were not marked on the bottom by the manufacturer, just count the measuring cupfuls of water (4 cups to the quart) that the casserole holds when it is brim-full. Then record this measure on the bottom with nail polish.*

CASSEROLED CORNED BEEF
(Pictured opposite)

5 to 5½ pounds corned-beef brisket	2 large onions, sliced
1 teaspoon whole peppercorns	3 cups diagonally-sliced celery
2 bay leaves	3 cups diagonally-sliced carrots
1 medium carrot, sliced	3 13¾-ounce cans chicken broth
1 large onion, sliced	1 tablespoon butter or margarine
1 teaspoon rosemary	Chili sauce
Few parsley sprigs	
3 cups sliced white potatoes	

Day before:
In large kettle place corned beef, peppercorns, bay leaves, sliced carrot, sliced onion, rosemary, and parsley sprigs. Cover with water. Bring to boil; simmer, covered, 3 hours, or until fork-tender. Drain; refrigerate meat.
About 2 hours before serving:
1. Start heating oven to 350°F.
2. Trim most of fat from corned beef. In 5-quart casserole, center corned beef, then surround, in layers, with sliced potatoes, onions, celery, and carrots, reserv-

ing a few pieces of onion and celery for later use. Add broth.
3. Bake, covered, 1 hour, or until vegetables are fork-tender.
4. Meanwhile, in butter, in skillet, sauté reserved celery and onion just until soft. Cover top of corned beef with chili sauce, then sprinkle on sautéed celery and onion.
5. Bake, uncovered, 20 minutes longer.
6. Serve, right from casserole, into open soup plates, slicing meat thinly. Serve with knife, fork, and soup spoon. Pass small bowl of prepared mustard, if desired. Makes 8 servings.

DINGLES' PORK-CHOP CASSEROLE

6 center-cut loin pork chops, ½ inch thick	2 cups milk
	¼ teaspoon salt
Seasoned salt	½ teaspoon orégano
1 tablespoon butter or margarine	¼ teaspoon marjoram
	¼ teaspoon thyme
1 large onion, chopped	⅓ cup snipped parsley
3 tablespoons regular all-purpose flour	

About 2 hours and 30 minutes before serving:
1. Start heating oven to 300°F.
2. Trim as much fat from pork chops as possible. Sprinkle chops well with seasoned salt. In hot skillet, brown quickly on both sides, then remove to 2-quart casserole.
3. In same skillet, in butter, sauté chopped onion until brown; stir in flour, then milk. When smooth and creamy, add salt, orégano, marjoram, thyme, and parsley. Pour over chops.
4. Bake, covered, 2 hours, or until very tender, stirring gravy twice.
5. Serve with stuffed mushrooms, parsleyed tomatoes, sweet potatoes, pear salad, and strawberry chiffon pie. Makes 6 servings.

PORK CHOPS RISOTTO

6 shoulder pork chops, ½ inch thick	1 or 2 green peppers
	Chili sauce
¾ teaspoon salt	1 envelope onion-soup mix
¼ teaspoon pepper	6 lemon slices
1 cup uncooked regular white rice	

About 1 hour and 30 minutes before serving:
1. Start heating oven to 350°F.
2. Trim pork chops of outside fat, then slit edges of each 3 or 4 times. Sprinkle with salt and pepper. In large skillet, over medium heat, brown chops well.
2. Spread bottom of 13-by-9-by-2-inch baking dish with rice; top rice with browned chops. On each chop

Casseroled Corned Beef

arrange a green-pepper ring, ½ inch thick, with a heaping teaspoon of chili sauce in the center of it.

3. Into drippings in skillet, pour 2½ cups water; stir in onion-soup mix; bring to boil, then pour into corner of baking dish.

4. Bake, covered, 1 hour, or until chops and rice are tender.

5. Serve each chop garnished with lemon slice. Makes 6 servings.

BAKED PORK CHOPS WITH MIXED BEANS

4 loin pork chops or shoulder steaks, ½ inch thick	½ teaspoon dry mustard
	1 1-pound 4-ounce can kidney beans, drained
Salt	1 1-pound 4-ounce can green limas, drained
Pepper	
¼ cup minced onion	¼ cup catchup
1 clove garlic, minced	2 tablespoons vinegar
1 teaspoon brown sugar	

1. Start heating oven to 350°F.
2. Trim a bit of fat from chops; in skillet, over low heat, heat piece of fat; then remove. Brown chops slowly in melted fat until rich golden brown on both sides — 15 to 20 minutes. (Spoon off excess fat as it accumulates.) Sprinkle chops with salt and pepper; set aside.
3. In drippings in skillet, sauté onion and garlic 5 minutes, or until tender. Stir in brown sugar, mustard, beans, catchup, and vinegar; mix well, season if necessary. Pour into 2-quart casserole. Arrange chops over beans.
4. Bake, covered, 45 minutes, or until chops are fork-tender. Makes 4 servings.

PORK-AND-VEGETABLE CASSEROLE

1 pound onions	1 cup cut-up green beans
¼ cup salad oil	1 carrot, sliced
1 pound boneless pork shoulder, cubed	2 cups diced green peppers
4 or 5 tomatoes, sliced ½ inch thick	2 cups pared, cubed eggplant
Salt	½ cup uncooked regular white rice
Pepper	¾ cup water

About 3 hours and 30 minutes before serving:
1. Slice onions thinly, then sauté in salad oil in skillet until soft; remove onions from skillet; in same skillet, sauté cubed pork until brown.
2. Start heating oven to 375°F.
3. On bottom of lightly oiled 12-by-8-by-2-inch baking dish arrange half of onions, then a layer of sliced tomatoes; sprinkle with 1 teaspoon salt and dash pepper; cover with half of beans, carrot, green peppers, and eggplant. Top with rice, then pork; sprinkle with 1

teaspoon salt and dash pepper; then top with rest of onions, beans, carrot, green peppers, eggplant, and tomatoes. Sprinkle with ½ teaspoon salt and dash pepper. Over all pour water and any oil left in skillet; cover with foil.

4. Bake 2 hours, removing foil for last 30 minutes. Makes 4 servings.

TRIPLE-TREAT CASSEROLE

3 tablespoons salad oil	Soy sauce
1 cup chopped onions	¼ teaspoon pepper
3 garlic cloves, minced	1 teaspoon paprika
1 pound boned pork shoulder, cut into ½-inch pieces	3 cups cooked rice
	2 canned pimentos, cut into strips
½ pound shrimp, cleaned, halved	2 hard-cooked eggs, sliced
1½ teaspoons salt	2 eggs, well beaten

About 1 hour and 30 minutes before serving:
1. In hot salad oil, in large skillet, sauté onions, garlic, and pork until lightly browned; add shrimp; sauté a few minutes longer. Toss in salt, 1 teaspoon soy sauce, pepper, paprika, and rice. Cool.
2. Start heating oven to 350°F.
3. In bottom of generously oiled 1½- or 2-quart casserole, arrange pimentos and sliced eggs.
4. Into cooled rice mixture toss, with fork, beaten eggs; turn into casserole; cover with foil. Set covered casserole in shallow baking pan containing about 1 inch hot water.
5. Bake 30 minutes.
6. Remove foil and unmold casserole on serving dish. Pass soy sauce. Makes 6 servings.

SCALLOPED HAM, POTATOES, AND CARROTS

1 thin center slice uncooked (cook-before-eating) ham (¾ pound)	1 cup milk
	3 cups thinly sliced, pared potatoes
2¼ teaspoons regular all-purpose flour	1 cup thinly sliced carrots
	¼ cup minced onion
1 10½-ounce can condensed cream-of-mushroom soup, undiluted	¾ teaspoon salt
	¼ teaspoon pepper

1. Start heating oven to 325°F.
2. In skillet, brown ham lightly on both sides; remove; cut into serving pieces. Stir flour into drippings left in skillet. Add soup, then slowly stir in milk. Heat, stirring, until boiling.
3. In 2-quart casserole, arrange layers of ham, potatoes, carrots, and onions until all are used, sprinkling vegetables with combined salt and pepper. Pour on soup mixture.

4. Bake, covered, 1 hour. Uncover; bake 15 minutes, or until potatoes and carrots are tender. Makes 3 or 4 servings.

PARTY STYLE: Double all ingredients. Use a 4-quart casserole. Bake, covered, 1 hour; uncover, and bake 30 minutes longer, or until potatoes and carrots are tender (or bake in two 2-quart casseroles as above). Makes 8 servings.

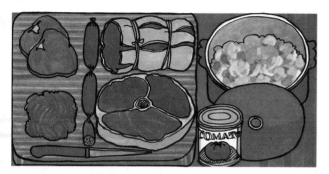

CHOUCROUTE À L'ALSACIENNE
(Pictured on page 14)

2 1-pound 11-ounce cans sauerkraut	¼ teaspoon whole peppercorns
1 1-pound can white potatoes	8 juniper berries (optional)
1 carrot, sliced	2 tablespoons instant minced onion
2 pounds smoked boneless shoulder butt	1 10½-ounce can condensed consommé, undiluted
¼ pound bacon, in 1 piece, or ½ pound sliced bacon	¾ to 1 cup white wine
3 bay leaves	4 knockwurst, or 6 frank-furters

About 2 hours and 45 minutes before serving:
1. Start heating oven to 400°F.
2. Drain and rinse sauerkraut; repeat if it seems salty. Place half of sauerkraut in shallow 4-quart casserole. Top with half of potatoes, drained; then half of carrot slices.
3. Cut smoked butt in ¾-inch crosswise slices; arrange half of them on top of carrots; cover with rest of sauerkraut. Repeat layering of smoked butt slices, potatoes, and carrots.
4. Place bacon, cut into ¼-inch slices, on top (or separate sliced bacon into 4 piles and arrange on top.) Tuck bay leaves in sauerkraut; sprinkle peppercorns, juniper berries, and instant minced onion over it. Pour consommé and 1 soup-can water over sauerkraut, then pour on wine. Cover casserole tightly with foil.
5. Bake casserole 2 hours. Remove paper-thin layer of skin from knockwurst (or use frankfurters as is), then arrange on top. Cover again with foil, and bake 30 minutes longer.

6. Serve with fresh rye bread, apple pie, apple strudel, or baked apples for dessert, and hot coffee. Makes 8 servings.

SWISS VEAL CASSEROLE

¼ cup regular all-purpose flour	2 medium onions, sliced
2 teaspoons salt	½ medium green pepper, slivered
⅛ teaspoon pepper	1 cup canned tomato juice
½ teaspoon monosodium glutamate	1 10-ounce package frozen lima beans, thawed just enough to separate
2-pound veal steak, 1 inch thick	
2 tablespoons salad oil	

Early on day:
1. Mix flour with 1 teaspoon salt, pepper, and mono-sodium glutamate; with edge of heavy saucer, pound this mixture into veal.
2. In hot salad oil, in skillet, sauté veal until well browned on both sides; remove to 10-by-6-by-2-inch baking dish.
3. In skillet, place onions and green pepper; stir, coating well with drippings; stir in tomato juice; then pour over veal. Refrigerate.

About 1 hour and 45 minutes before serving:
1. Start heating oven to 350°F.
2. Cover baking dish containing veal with foil.
3. Bake 40 minutes. Arrange lima beans around veal. Sprinkle with 1 teaspoon salt. Bake, covered, 45 minutes longer, or until veal is fork-tender. Makes 4 servings.

LANCASHIRE HOT POT

6 round bone shoulder lamb chops	6 medium potatoes, pared, thinly sliced
2½ teaspoons salt	2 medium onions, sliced
½ teaspoon pepper	¼ pound fresh mushrooms, sliced, or 1 3- or 4-ounce can sliced mushrooms, drained
½ teaspoon thyme leaves	
1 tablespoon butter or margarine	
3 lamb kidneys, sliced	1 tablespoon regular all-purpose flour

About 2 hours before serving:
1. Trim fat and remove bones from chops. Place fat and bones in medium saucepan; add 1¼ cups water and ½ teaspoon salt. Simmer, covered, 30 minutes; then strain off 1 cup broth.
2. Start heating oven to 375°F.
3. Mix 2 teaspoons salt, pepper, and thyme; sprinkle half of it on chops. In large skillet, melt butter; sauté lamb chops and kidneys until brown.
4. In greased 3-quart casserole arrange layer of potato slices; sprinkle with some of thyme mixture, then top

Choucroute à l'Alsacienne

Lamb Chop Casserole

with some of onion and mushroom slices, 3 chops, and half of kidney slices. Repeat layers, topping with potato slices. Into skillet, stir flour, then broth. Bring to boil; pour over potato slices. Cover casserole.

5. Bake 45 minutes, then uncover and bake 30 minutes longer, or until potatoes are tender. Sprinkle with snipped parsley, if desired. Makes 6 servings.

LAMB CHOP CASSEROLE
(Pictured opposite)

1 pound small white onions (about 18)	½ lemon
12 loin lamb chops, ¾ inch thick	1 pound cooked or canned whole young carrots
Onion salt	1 10-ounce jar currant jelly
3 large baking apples	

Day before, or early on day:
1. In boiling salted water, in medium saucepan, cook onions, covered, until almost tender.
2. Meanwhile, sprinkle chops with onion salt; then, in large skillet, brown chops on both sides.
3. Halve, core, then rub cut surface of apples with lemon half.
4. Around sides of large shallow casserole, stand 10 chops; lay 2 more on bottom; then arrange apple halves, onions, and carrots as pictured.
5. In small saucepan, melt half of jelly. Spoon over casserole; cover with saran and refrigerate.

About 30 minutes before serving:
1. Start heating oven to 350°F.
2. Bake casserole about 30 minutes, or until apples are tender and all are glazed, brushing once or twice during baking with rest of jelly, melted. Makes 6 servings.

SWEET-AND-SOUR LIVER

6 slices bacon, diced	¼ teaspoon marjoram
1 small onion, chopped	¼ teaspoon crumbled rosemary
½ green pepper, chopped	
½ cup dark-brown sugar, packed	½ teaspoon monosodium glutamate
½ cup white vinegar	1½ pounds beef liver, in slices 2 to 3 inches wide
1 teaspoon salt	
⅛ teaspoon pepper	

About 50 minutes before serving:
1. Start heating oven to 350°F.
2. In medium skillet, over medium heat, cook bacon until light brown; add onion and green pepper; cook until tender—about 5 minutes. Add brown sugar, vinegar, salt, pepper, marjoram, rosemary, and monosodium glutamate.
3. Cut membrane from liver; lay liver slices in 13-by-9-by-2-inch baking dish; pour on sauce.

4. Bake 25 minutes.
5. Serve with parsley rice, buttered baby carrots, tossed salad, and fresh fruit for dessert. Makes 4 to 6 servings.

FILLED SAUSAGE RING

1 13-ounce Polish sausage	Prepared mustard
1 or 2 crisp apples, pared, cut in thin wedges	1 10-ounce package frozen peas, thawed
1 or 2 firm tomatoes, cut in thin wedges	¼ teaspoon salt
3 or 4 process Cheddar-cheese slices, quartered	1 tablespoon butter or margarine

About 1 hour before serving:
1. Start heating oven to 375°F.
2. With sharp knife, make crosswise cuts in sausage, ½-inch apart, and three fourths the way through. Lay sausage in ring in buttered 11-inch pie plate or shallow baking dish.
3. Prepare apples, tomatoes, and cheese slices. Spread tomato wedges with mustard. In sausage slits, alternate cheese slices, apple and tomato wedges. Heap peas in center; add salt and butter.
4. Bake 25 minutes, or until peas are hot, basting with drippings.
5. Serve sausage ring with stuffed baked potatoes, rhubarb pie with sour cream, and coffee. Makes 4 servings.

EGGPLANT-SAUSAGE BAKE

1 medium eggplant, cut into ½- to 1-inch cubes	1 teaspoon salt
2 fresh tomatoes, cut into pieces*	⅛ teaspoon pepper
	2 cups water
¼ pound fresh mushrooms, quartered*	1 pound sweet Italian sausage
2 tablespoons onion-soup mix	5 slices white bread
	Butter or margarine
1½ teaspoons orégano	Grated Parmesan cheese
2 teaspoons monosodium glutamate	Paprika
	Snipped parsley

About 1 hour before serving:
1. In 3-quart saucepan combine eggplant, tomatoes, and mushrooms. Add onion-soup mix, orégano, monosodium glutamate, salt, pepper, and water. Boil, uncovered, stirring occasionally, about 35 minutes, or until eggplant and tomatoes lose their shape and mixture is thick.
2. Meanwhile, in medium skillet, sauté sausage until well browned; drain on paper towels. Cut into 1-inch slices.
3. Start heating oven to 375°F.
4. Butter one side of bread slices; cut into ½-inch cubes.

5. When vegetable mixture is done, add sausage slices; pour into 2-quart round casserole. Top with bread cubes; sprinkle generously with cheese; dust lightly with paprika.

6. Bake 25 to 30 minutes, or until golden.

7. Sprinkle ring of snipped parsley around outer edge. Serve with deviled-egg salad, finger rolls, and gingerbread with hot lemon sauce for dessert. Makes 6 servings.

*A 1-pound can stewed tomatoes and a 3- or 4-ounce can mushroom pieces and stems with their liquid may be substituted for tomatoes and mushrooms; reduce water to 1 cup.

APPLE-SAUSAGE BAKE
(Pictured opposite)

2 pounds bulk pork sausage meat	1 package (4-serving size) instant mashed potatoes
3 medium red apples, unpared	¼ teaspoon pepper
Cinnamon	3 egg yolks, unbeaten
	3 egg whites, unbeaten
	Melted butter or margarine

About 2 hours before serving:

1. Cut pork sausage meat into about ½-inch slices; then sauté, in medium skillet, over medium heat, until well browned on all sides, pouring off fat as it accumulates. Drain sausage slices on paper towels; cut into small pieces, then arrange over bottom of ungreased 2½-quart casserole.

2. Core apples; cut into slices about ½-inch thick. Stand a ring of apple slices on top of sausage slices around edge of casserole as pictured. Pile rest of apple slices in center of casserole. Sprinkle generously with cinnamon.

3. Start heating oven to 350°F.

4. Make up mashed potatoes as package label directs, adding pepper and egg yolks. In small bowl, with mixer at high speed, beat egg whites until stiff but not dry. Fold into slightly cooled potato mixture, then pile in center of casserole. With tip of paring knife, trace a series of swirls in potatoes; brush top gently with melted butter.

5. Bake casserole 50 to 60 minutes, or until apple slices test done.

6. Serve, cut into wedges with sharp knife, using a pie server for serving. Nice with tomato bouillon and cheese crackers, Brussels sprouts, and chocolate pudding. Makes 6 servings.

FOR 4: About 1½ hours before serving, start making casserole using 1 pound sausage, 2 apples, cinnamon, 1 package instant mashed potatoes, ¼ teaspoon pepper, and 2 eggs. Prepare as above in 1½-quart casserole; bake 45 minutes, or until done, with piece of foil underneath casserole.

TOP-HATTER FRANKS

2 tablespoons butter or margarine	2 tablespoons prepared mustard
1 medium onion, minced	1 10½-ounce can condensed bean-and-bacon soup, undiluted
1 green pepper, sliced	
½ cup minced celery	1 soup-can milk, or diluted evaporated milk
1 pound frankfurters, sliced ½ inch thick	1 package corn-muffin mix

1. Start heating oven to 350°F.

2. In hot butter, in skillet, sauté onion, green pepper, and celery until tender. Stir in frankfurters, mustard, soup, and milk. Turn mixture into 12-by-8-by-2-inch baking dish.

3. Prepare corn-muffin mix as package label directs; pour over frank mixture.

4. Bake 35 minutes, or until corn-muffin mix is done. Makes 8 servings.

MAMMY'S WAY: Substitute the following corn-bread batter for corn-muffin mix: Into mixing bowl, sift 1 cup corn meal, ¼ cup sifted regular all-purpose flour, 2 tablespoons granulated sugar, ½ teaspoon salt, and 1½ teaspoons double-acting baking powder. Add 2 tablespoons salad oil, 1 egg, and ½ cup milk. With hand beater, beat until smooth—about 1 minute. Pour over frank mixture; bake as above.

GRETCHEN'S CASSEROLE

1 1-pound or 1-pound 4-ounce can sauerkraut	2 tablespoons butter or margarine
1 1-pound 4-ounce can apple slices	2 12-ounce cans luncheon meat
⅓ cup brown sugar, firmly packed	¼ cup brown sugar, firmly packed
2 tablespoons vinegar	2 teaspoons prepared mustard
¼ cup minced onion	

1. Start heating oven to 400°F.

2. In 2-quart casserole combine sauerkraut and apples, undrained, with ⅓ cup brown sugar, vinegar, and onion; dot with butter.

3. With sharp knife, slice luncheon meat into 8 to 12 slices; arrange on top of sauerkraut mixture. Combine ¼ cup brown sugar with mustard; spread evenly on meat slices.

4. Bake, uncovered, 30 to 40 minutes, or until meat is glazed and sauerkraut is heated through. Makes 4 to 6 servings.

FOR 2: Use 1¼ cups canned sauerkraut, 1¼ cups canned apple slices, 2½ tablespoons brown sugar, 1 tablespoon vinegar, 2 tablespoons minced onion, 1 tablespoon butter or margarine, 1 can luncheon meat, 2 tablespoons brown sugar, and 1 teaspoon prepared mustard. Bake in 1-quart casserole.

Sea-Stuffed Peppers, Apple-Sausage Bake

SESAME POLYNESIAN CHICKEN

¼ cup butter or margarine	1 small onion, thinly sliced
1 2- to 2½-pound broiler-fryer, cut up	⅓ cup sliced stuffed olives
½ cup regular all-purpose flour	1 7-ounce package frozen shrimp
2 teaspoons salt	1 10¾-ounce can condensed tomato soup, undiluted
¼ teaspoon pepper	
1 13½-ounce can pineapple chunks	¼ cup chili sauce
1 small green pepper, thinly sliced	¼ cup canned pineapple syrup or water
	1 can refrigerated sesame dinner rolls

1. Start heating oven to 375°F.
2. In 13-by-9-by-2-inch baking pan melt butter. Roll chicken pieces in mixture of flour, salt, and pepper, then place, skin side down, in pan.
3. Bake 30 minutes.
4. Drain pineapple chunks, reserving syrup. Turn chicken pieces, then top with green pepper and onion rings, olives, and pineapple chunks. Rinse shrimp in cold water until ice coating is removed; add to chicken. Combine soup, chili sauce, and reserved pineapple syrup; pour over chicken. Cover pan with foil.
5. Bake 30 minutes.
6. Now cut each sesame roll into 4 pieces, making tiny sesame squares; arrange on top of chicken. Bake, uncovered, 15 minutes, or until rolls are golden brown. Serve hot. Makes 4 to 6 servings.

OCEANIA CHICKEN

1 2½- to 3-pound broiler-fryer, cut up	½ teaspoon nutmeg
⅔ cup regular all-purpose flour	¼ cup butter or margarine
1 teaspoon salt	1 1-pound 4-ounce can sliced pineapple
½ teaspoon celery salt	½ cup soy sauce
½ teaspoon garlic salt	2 tablespoons granulated sugar

Day before:
1. Wipe chicken pieces; pat dry with paper towels.
2. Start heating oven to 350°F.
3. Mix flour, salt, celery salt, garlic salt, and nutmeg in paper or plastic bag; shake chicken pieces in flour mixture to coat well on all sides.
4. In hot butter, in large skillet, brown chicken on all sides. Place chicken pieces in 2½-quart casserole.

Set skillet aside, without draining any remaining butter, for use in step 7.
5. Combine syrup from canned pineapple with soy sauce and sugar. Pour over chicken pieces; cover casserole.
6. Bake about 1 hour, or until chicken is tender, basting several times.
7. Meanwhile, sauté pineapple slices in butter left in skillet (add more butter if needed), until golden on both sides. Fifteen minutes before chicken is done, top with pineapple slices.
8. Cool a little, then refrigerate.
About 30 minutes before serving:
Reheat chicken at 350°F. about 30 minutes, or until heated through, basting twice. Serve with Polynesian Rice Mingle, page 41, garden spinach, and baked frozen-raspberry tarts. Makes 4 to 6 servings.
Note: If more convenient, entire dish may be prepared just before serving, allowing about 1 hour and 30 minutes.

CHICKEN WITH CRAB-MEAT STUFFING

2 2- to 2½-pound broiler-fryers, split in halves	¼ cup sherry
2 tablespoons soft butter or margarine	¼ cup catchup
	1 3- or 4-ounce can sliced or button mushrooms, drained (optional)
1 teaspoon salt	
¼ teaspoon pepper	½ teaspoon garlic salt
Paprika (optional)	Parsley sprigs (optional)
¼ cup melted butter or margarine	1 tomato, sliced (optional)
	Crab-Meat Stuffing, below

About 1 hour and 45 minutes before serving:
1. Start heating oven to 350°F.
2. Rub chicken halves with soft butter, salt, and pepper; sprinkle with paprika, if desired. In 13-by-9-by-2-inch baking dish, side by side, arrange chicken halves with wings tucked back and under, and skin side up.
3. Bake 35 minutes.
4. Meanwhile, in small saucepan combine melted butter, sherry, catchup, mushrooms, and garlic salt; heat. Over each chicken half spoon 1 or 2 tablespoons of this butter sauce. Bake chicken 10 minutes longer.
5. Remove from oven and let cool in baking dish while preparing Crab-Meat Stuffing.
6. Now turn chicken halves over; generously fill each "shell" with stuffing, then baste each with 1 or 2 tablespoons butter sauce.
7. Bake 30 to 35 minutes, basting with rest of butter sauce.
8. When chicken is fork-tender, remove from oven; garnish here and there with bits of parsley and in center with sliced tomato, if desired. Serve stuffing side up. Makes 4 servings.
CRAB-MEAT STUFFING: Cut 3 slices white bread into

small cubes. In medium bowl toss bread cubes with 5 tablespoons light cream or milk until all liquid is absorbed. Remove membrane from 2 6-ounce packages frozen crab meat, thawed, drained, or 2 6½-ounce cans King-crab meat, drained; toss with bread cubes. Into ¼ cup melted butter or margarine stir ¼ teaspoon cayenne pepper, 1 teaspoon salt, 1 teaspoon prepared mustard, ½ teaspoon thyme, ½ teaspoon poultry seasoning, and ¼ teaspoon sage (optional). Add to bread and crab-meat mixture. Toss all together lightly with fork. Use to fill 4 chicken halves.

CASSEROLE-BARBECUED CHICKEN

1 3- to 3½-pound roasting chicken, cut up	1 cup water
½ cup regular all-purpose flour	2 tablespoons Worcestershire
2 teaspoons salt	1 tablespoon brown sugar
¼ cup salad oil or fat	⅛ teaspoon pepper
1 medium onion, sliced	1 10-ounce package frozen whole-kernel corn, thawed just enough to separate
½ cup chopped celery	
¼ cup minced green pepper	
1 cup catchup	

Early on day:
1. Dip chicken pieces into flour mixed with salt. In hot oil, in skillet, sauté chicken until golden on all sides; remove to 2½-quart casserole.
2. Pour all but 1 tablespoon oil from skillet; to oil in skillet add onion, then sauté until golden and tender. Stir in celery, green pepper, catchup, water, Worcestershire, brown sugar, and pepper; pour over chicken; refrigerate.

About 2 hours before serving:
1. Start heating oven to 350°F.
2. Bake chicken, covered, 1 hour and 20 minutes. Add corn and bake, covered, 25 minutes longer, or until chicken is tender. Makes 6 servings.

MEXICAN CHICKEN CASSEROLE

1 4- to 5-pound roasting chicken, cut up	24 pitted ripe olives (about 1 cup)
1 stalk celery, cut up	½ teaspoon garlic salt
1 bay leaf	1 teaspoon salt
2 teaspoons salt	¼ teaspoon sage
2 tablespoons shortening	½ teaspoon seasoned pepper
2 small onions, chopped	
1 green pepper, chopped	1 12-ounce can whole-kernel corn, drained
¼ cup regular all-purpose flour	¼ teaspoon seasoned salt
1 1-pound can tomatoes	

Day before, or early on day:
1. In large saucepan or Dutch oven, over low heat, simmer chicken with celery, bay leaf, and 2 teaspoons salt, in just enough water to cover, covered, until tender—about 1½ hours. Remove chicken from broth; cool; refrigerate chicken and broth.

About 1 hour and 15 minutes before serving:
1. Start heating oven to 350°F.
2. Remove sizeable pieces of chicken from bones; remove skin.
3. In shortening, in medium skillet, sauté onions and green pepper 5 minutes; stir in flour, then tomatoes, olives, garlic salt, 1 teaspoon salt, sage, and seasoned pepper.
4. Arrange half of corn in greased 2-quart casserole; sprinkle with half of seasoned salt; top with half of chicken pieces and olive sauce. Repeat.
5. Bake 40 minutes. Makes 8 servings.

CHICKEN CASSEROLE DE LUXE

1 4-pound roasting chicken	½ soup-can chicken broth
1 tablespoon salt	½ teaspoon dry onion flakes
3 cups seasoned, cooked green beans	¼ cup slivered almonds or fresh mushrooms (optional)
20 single saltines	
1 cup shredded process Cheddar cheese	1 tablespoon melted butter or margarine
1 10½-ounce can condensed cream-of-chicken soup, undiluted	

Make early on day, or about 2 hours before serving:
1. Wash chicken; place in large kettle with 2 quarts boiling water and salt. Simmer, covered, until tender—about 1 hour. Drain, reserving broth; cool; remove chicken meat from bones.
2. Start heating oven to 350°F.
3. Arrange beans over bottom of greased 13-by-9-by-2-inch baking dish; arrange half of chicken meat over beans. Top with 16 of the saltines, then half of cheese, then remaining chicken meat.
4. Combine soup, broth, onion flakes, and remaining cheese; pour over chicken. Crumble remaining saltines; sprinkle over casserole with almonds. Drizzle with melted butter.

Herb-Dumpling Chicken Pie

Golden Fricassee

5. Bake about 30 minutes, or until bubbling hot and lightly browned. Or refrigerate, then start baking about 30 minutes before serving.

6. Serve with shrimp cocktail, romaine salad, buttered pumpernickel, and coffee. Makes 6 servings.

HERB-DUMPLING CHICKEN PIE
(Pictured opposite)

1 4½- to 6-pound stewing chicken, cut up	2¼ cups sifted regular all-purpose flour
1 whole carrot	4 teaspoons double-acting baking powder
¾ pound small white onions	
1 celery stalk	1 teaspoon poultry seasoning
1 whole clove	
1 whole peppercorn	1 teaspoon celery seeds
Salt	2 teaspoons poppy seeds
2 cups diagonally sliced carrots	1 teaspoon instant minced onion
¼ cup regular all-purpose flour	¼ cup salad oil
1 teaspoon paprika	½ cup evaporated milk, diluted with ½ cup water
1 10½-ounce can condensed cream-of-chicken soup, undiluted	¼ cup melted butter or margarine
1 10-ounce package frozen peas, or 1 16- or 17-ounce can peas, drained	1¾ cups fresh bread crumbs

Day before, or early on day:
1. In large Dutch oven, place chicken; cover with hot water, then add whole carrot, 1 onion, celery stalk, clove, peppercorn, and 2 teaspoons salt. Cover; simmer 1 hour and 30 minutes, or until fork-tender.
2. Remove chicken and vegetables from broth. Remove chicken meat from bones in large pieces. Measure broth, adding water if needed, to make 3 cups. Refrigerate chicken and broth.

About 1 hour and 15 minutes before serving:
1. In Dutch oven, in chicken broth, simmer, covered, rest of onions and sliced carrots 12 to 15 minutes, or until tender-crisp.
2. Combine ¼ cup flour and paprika. Stir in enough chicken broth from Dutch oven to make a smooth paste, then stir into rest of broth and vegetables. Cook until smooth and thickened, stirring constantly. Stir in soup until blended.
3. Start heating oven to 425°F.
4. To thickened broth add chicken meat and peas. Heat until very hot and bubbly, stirring occasionally.
5. Meanwhile, into bowl sift 2 cups flour with baking powder, ½ teaspoon salt, poultry seasoning, celery and poppy seeds. Add instant minced onion, salad oil, and evaporated milk; stir until just moistened. Mix melted butter with bread crumbs.
6. Transfer hot, bubbly chicken mixture to 3-quart casserole. Drop rounded tablespoonfuls of herb-dumpling dough in crumb mixture; roll to coat well with crumbs. Arrange dumplings in circle around outer edge of casserole.
7. Bake 25 to 30 minutes, or until dumplings test done.
8. Nice served with chilled canned fruit cocktail plus lemon juice, over split bananas, and hot coffee. Makes 6 to 8 servings.

GOLDEN FRICASSEE
(Pictured opposite)

1 4½- to 5-pound roasting chicken, cut up	½ pound fresh mushrooms, sliced
Salt	½ cup regular all-purpose flour
Pepper	
Paprika	¼ teaspoon mace
Butter or margarine	¼ teaspoon nutmeg
1 medium onion, sliced	½ cup sherry (optional)
1 carrot, sliced	1 cup commercial sour cream
2 bay leaves	
2 pounds small white onions	Snipped parsley (optional)

About 2 hours before serving:
1. Sprinkle chicken with ½ teaspoon salt, pepper, and paprika. In ¼ cup butter, in large skillet, sauté chicken until golden. Add sliced onion, carrot, bay leaves, and 1 quart water. Cook, covered, 50 minutes, or until fork-tender.
2. Meanwhile, in ¼ cup butter, in another skillet, sauté onions until golden; then add ½ cup water and cook, covered, 15 to 20 minutes, or until fork-tender. Remove; keep warm.
3. In 2 tablespoons butter, in same skillet, sauté mushrooms until just soft; keep warm.
4. In small bowl blend together ½ cup butter, flour, mace, nutmeg, and 1 teaspoon salt.
5. Start heating oven to 350°F.
6. When chicken is tender, arrange in 4-quart casserole, along with onions and mushrooms. Strain broth in which chicken cooked, then return 3½ cups of it to large skillet. Add sherry or another ½ cup broth; into it stir flour mixture; cook, stirring constantly, until slightly thickened. Remove from heat and gradually stir in sour cream; pour over chicken.
7. Bake casserole, covered, 30 minutes.
8. Serve at once, garnished with parsley, if desired. Nice with cranberry juice cocktail, broccoli, toasted corn muffins, peach Melba, and coffee. Makes 6 to 8 servings.
Note: To do a day ahead, make fricassee as in steps 1 through 6. Refrigerate, covered, overnight. To prepare for serving, remove any fat from surface, then bake, covered, 1 hour and 45 minutes, or until hot and bubbly.

CURRY-CHICKEN DIVAN

3 whole, boned chicken
  breasts
1 carrot, sliced
1 small onion, chopped
1 teaspoon salt
2 10-ounce packages frozen
  broccoli spears
1 10½-ounce can
  condensed cream-of-
  chicken soup, undiluted
⅔ cup mayonnaise or
  salad dressing

⅓ cup undiluted evaporated
  milk
½ cup grated process
  Cheddar cheese
1 teaspoon lemon juice
½ teaspoon curry powder
1 tablespoon melted
  butter or margarine
½ cup packaged dried
  bread crumbs

About 2 hours before serving:

1. In kettle place chicken breasts, carrot, and onion; add hot water to cover and 1 teaspoon salt. Cook, covered, about 45 minutes, or until chicken is tender; drain. Cut each chicken breast into quarters.
2. Cook broccoli as package label directs, until almost tender; drain.
3. Start heating oven to 350°F.
4. Arrange broccoli in greased 2-quart casserole; top with chicken-breast quarters.
5. In bowl mix soup, mayonnaise, evaporated milk, cheese, lemon juice, and curry powder; pour over chicken. Mix melted butter with bread crumbs; sprinkle over sauce.
6. Bake 30 minutes, or until heated. Makes 6 to 8 servings.

CHEESY CHICKEN CASSEROLE

1 4-pound stewing chicken,
  or 6 chicken breasts
2 10-ounce packages
  frozen broccoli spears
2 cups milk

2 8-ounce packages cream
  cheese
1 teaspoon salt
¾ to 1 teaspoon garlic salt
1½ cups shredded
  Parmesan cheese

Early on day:

Gently simmer whole chicken or chicken breasts in salted boiling water just to cover, 1 to 1½ hours, or until tender. Remove chicken; let cool; then remove skin. Thinly slice chicken; cover with wax paper and refrigerate.

About 1 hour before serving:

1. Start heating oven to 350°F.
2. Cook broccoli as package label directs. Cut each broccoli spear into bite-size pieces; arrange in bottom of greased 2-quart oblong casserole.
3. In double boiler blend milk, cream cheese, salt, and garlic salt until smooth and hot. Stir in ¾ cup shredded cheese until smooth.
4. Pour 1 cup sauce mixture over broccoli; top with all of sliced chicken, in one layer. Cover chicken with

rest of sauce. Sprinkle ¼ cup shredded cheese over top.
5. Bake 25 to 30 minutes, or until piping hot.
6. Remove from oven; let stand 5 to 10 minutes. Serve sprinkled with rest of shredded cheese. Makes 6 to 8 servings.

FOR 3: Make half of recipe above, using 1½-quart casserole.

CRISP-CRUSTED CHICKEN CASSEROLE
(Pictured opposite)

1 4-pound roasting chicken,
  cut up
Salt
1 teaspoon whole
  peppercorns
1 bay leaf
1 large onion, quartered
2 celery stalks, halved
3 cups packaged precooked
  long-grain rice
1½ teaspoons granulated
  sugar
½ teaspoon mace
¼ cup butter or margarine
1 cup chopped unblanched
  almonds

¼ cup regular all-purpose
  flour
½ cup canned tomato
  sauce
1 10-ounce package frozen
  mixed vegetables,
  thawed
¼ cup diced canned
  pimentos
1 4-ounce can mushroom
  pieces and stems,
  undrained
3 eggs, unbeaten
Canned slivered blanched
  almonds

Day before, or early on day:

1. In large covered kettle, simmer chicken in 1½ quarts cold water, with 2 tablespoons salt, peppercorns, bay leaf, onion, and celery stalks, 1½ to 2 hours, or until chicken is fork-tender.
2. Remove chicken from kettle; cool slightly. Strain broth; cool; refrigerate. Meanwhile, carefully remove skin, then cut chicken from bones in chunks. Wrap; refrigerate.

About 1 hour and 30 minutes before serving:

1. Cook rice as package label directs; remove from heat; add sugar, mace, butter, and chopped almonds; cool.
2. Meanwhile, in large saucepan heat 2½ cups chicken broth. Combine flour with 1 teaspoon salt; stir gradually into chicken broth. Add tomato sauce and stir over medium-high heat until mixture boils. Remove from heat; stir in chicken chunks, mixed vegetables, pimentos, and mushrooms. Pour into 2½-quart casserole.
3. Start heating oven to 350°F.
4. Beat eggs well; carefully fold in cooled rice mixture; spread over top of casserole, leaving a small hole in center for steam to escape. Stick slivered almonds, at random, into rice mixture.
5. Bake 1 hour.
6. Serve hot, right from casserole. Nice with spiced peaches. Makes 6 to 8 servings.

FLORENTINE CHICKEN

1 10-ounce package frozen
   chopped spinach
Butter or margarine
3 tablespoons regular all-
   purpose flour
1 teaspoon monosodium
   glutamate
1 teaspoon salt
Dash cayenne pepper

1½ cups milk
¼ cup grated Parmesan
   cheese
½ cup light cream
2 cups cooked chicken, in
   chunks
¼ cup packaged dried
   bread crumbs

Early on day:

1. Cook spinach as package label directs; drain well, then arrange in 1½-quart casserole.

2. In saucepan, melt 2 tablespoons butter. Stir in flour, monosodium glutamate, salt, and cayenne. Gradually stir in milk; cook, stirring constantly, until mixture is thickened and comes to boil.

3. Add cheese and cream. Stir, over low heat, until cheese melts; add chicken and pour over spinach. Sprinkle with bread crumbs; refrigerate.

About 30 minutes before serving:

1. Start heating oven to 350°F.

2. Dot casserole with butter.

3. Bake 15 minutes, then set under broiler to lightly brown top. Makes 4 servings.

CHICKEN BAKE

2 eggs, beaten
½ cup milk
2 cups fresh bread crumbs
1 onion, chopped
2 tablespoons snipped
   parsley
¼ teaspoon thyme

¾ teaspoon seasoned salt
½ teaspoon salt
⅛ teaspoon pepper
1 cup cut-up cooked
   chicken
One of sauces, page 24

About 1 hour before serving:

1. Start heating oven to 350°F.

Crisp-Crusted Chicken Casserole

2. Mix together all ingredients except sauce. Pour into greased 1-quart casserole.

3. Bake 45 minutes, or until firm.

4. Let stand a few minutes; loosen edges with spatula, invert serving dish on top, then invert both and lift off casserole. Serve with sauce over top. Makes 3 servings.

SOUR CREAM SAUCE: In small saucepan combine ½ cup mayonnaise, ½ cup commercial sour cream, ½ teaspoon prepared mustard, and 3 tablespoons snipped parsley; heat, stirring, then serve.

CELERY SAUCE: Combine ½ 10½-ounce can condensed cream-of-celery soup, undiluted, ¼ cup milk, and 1 tablespoon snipped parsley; bring to boiling, stirring, then serve.

CHICKEN-AND-DRESSING CASSEROLE

1 4-pound roasting chicken, cut up	¼ cup coarsely chopped celery
3 cups hot water	1 teaspoon salt
1 clove-studded onion	¼ teaspoon pepper
1 tablespoon salt	¼ teaspoon poultry seasoning
1 bay leaf	
1 carrot	2 cups chicken broth
4 cups large toasted bread cubes	2 tablespoons regular all-purpose flour
1 medium onion, minced	

Early on day:

1. In large kettle place chicken, hot water, clove-studded onion, 1 tablespoon salt, bay leaf, and carrot. Cook, covered, about 1½ hours, or until chicken is tender. Cool chicken and broth; remove chicken meat in large chunks.

2. Make dressing by combining bread cubes, minced onion, celery, 1 teaspoon salt, pepper, poultry seasoning, and 1 cup chicken broth.

3. Start heating oven to 350°F.

4. Arrange half of chicken meat in 13-by-9-by-2-inch baking dish or 2-quart casserole; top with half of dressing; repeat.

5. In saucepan mix flour with ¼ cup broth until smooth; slowly stir in remaining ¾ cup broth. Cook,

stirring, until thickened; pour over chicken mixture.

6. Bake 25 minutes, or until bubbly.

7. Serve with green beans almondine, raw carrot strips, and melon à la mode. Makes 8 servings.

CHICKEN-CHEESE PUFF

Butter or margarine	2 egg yolks, unbeaten
6 tablespoons regular all-purpose flour	1 cup cut-up cooked chicken, or 1 5½- or 6-ounce can chicken
1½ cups milk	
1 teaspoon seasoned salt	3 bread slices
⅛ teaspoon nutmeg	2 egg whites, unbeaten
½ cup grated process Cheddar cheese	

About 1 hour and 30 minutes before serving:

1. Melt 2 tablespoons butter; stir in flour, then gradually stir in milk. Cook, stirring, until thickened. Remove from heat; add seasoned salt, nutmeg, cheese, and egg yolks, stirring until smooth. Now add chicken; mix well.

2. Start heating oven to 350°F.

3. Butter bread slices; lay 1 slice, buttered-side down, on bottom of 1-quart casserole; halve other slices and use to line sides.

4. Beat egg whites until stiff; fold into chicken mixture; pour over bread.

5. Bake 1 hour, or until golden and puffy.

6. Serve at once. Makes 2 or 3 servings.

ASPARAGUS-CHICKEN CASSEROLE

1 10-ounce package frozen asparagus spears	½ teaspoon paprika
	½ teaspoon basil
Butter or margarine	1 cup milk
1 small onion, chopped	1 tablespoon sherry
1 3- or 4-ounce can sliced mushrooms	1 cup cut-up cooked chicken, or 1 5½- or 6-ounce can chicken
2 tablespoons regular all-purpose flour	
	2 slices toast
¾ teaspoon seasoned salt	

About 40 minutes before serving:

1. Start heating oven to 400°F.

2. Cook asparagus as package label directs.

3. In 1½ tablespoons hot butter, in medium saucepan, lightly brown onion and drained mushrooms (reserve liquid).

3. Stir in flour, seasoned salt, paprika, and basil; gradually add milk and mushroom liquid. Cook, stirring, until thickened; add sherry and chicken.

4. Lay toast slices in 10-by-6-by-2-inch baking dish; top with asparagus; dot with butter. Pour chicken around them.

5. Bake 10 minutes, or until bubbly. Makes 2 or 3 servings.

Fish and Shellfish Casseroles

SEA-FOOD FILLETS

1½ pounds flounder
   fillets
¾ teaspoon salt
Dash pepper
¾ cup milk

1 can frozen cream-of-
   shrimp soup
1 cup grated sharp cheese
3 tablespoons sherry
Paprika

1. Start heating oven to 350°F.
2. Roll up each fillet. Stand them up in 10-by-6-by-2-inch baking dish; sprinkle with salt and pepper. Pour milk over fish.
3. Bake, uncovered, 30 minutes; then remove from oven, drain milk off and reserve.
4. Thaw shrimp soup as label directs; mix with reserved milk; heat, stirring until hot and smooth. Add ¾ cup grated cheese; stir until melted. Add sherry; pour over fish. Top with rest of grated cheese; sprinkle with paprika.
5. Brown under broiler. Makes 4 servings.

FISH WITH A BOUQUET OF VEGETABLES
(Pictured on page 2)

About 3 cups cooked rice
Salt
¼ cup olive oil
2 cloves garlic, minced
½ pound small white
   onions
2 medium green peppers,
   cut into 1½-inch pieces
1½ pounds zucchini,
   unpared, cut into 1-inch
   diagonal slices
1 teaspoon regular all-
   purpose flour

1 teaspoon basil
½ teaspoon orégano
⅛ teaspoon pepper
Seasoned salt
½ cup dry white wine
6 large flounder fillets
6 slices natural Swiss
   cheese
2 tablespoons butter or
   margarine
Few radish roses
6 lemon wedges
Few sprigs fresh dill

About 1 hour and 30 minutes before serving:
1. Cook rice as package label directs, using ½ teaspoon salt and omitting butter. Arrange along center of 13-by-9-by-2-inch baking dish to within 2 inches of edges.
2. Start heating oven to 350°F.
3. In large skillet heat olive oil; add garlic, onions, green peppers, and zucchini; sauté 5 minutes. Sprinkle with flour, basil, orégano, pepper, 1¼ teaspoons salt,

and 1 teaspoon seasoned salt. Add 1 cup water and white wine; bring to boil, covered, then simmer 10 minutes.
4. Around rice in baking dish arrange zucchini mixture, with juices. Sprinkle fillets with ¾ teaspoon salt and ¾ teaspoon seasoned salt. Fold one end of each fillet over about one third of the way; fold cheese slices in half crosswise. Then arrange fillets and cheese, alternately, over rice. Dot with butter.
5. Bake 15 minutes; then increase oven heat to 400°F. and bake 15 minutes longer, or until fish is done and cheese is melted and golden.
6. Serve garnished with radish roses, lemon wedges, and fresh dill sprigs as pictured on page 2. Makes 6 servings.

FISH AND FRENCH FRIES
(Pictured on page 26)

8 frozen fish fillets,
   thawed
½ cup snipped parsley
1½ teaspoons salt
¼ teaspoon pepper

Frozen French fries
1 16- or 17-ounce can
   stewed tomatoes
   (2 cups)
½ cup snipped parsley

1. Start heating oven to 350°F.
2. Sprinkle fillets with ½ cup parsley, salt, and pepper. Top each fillet with 5 or 6 French fries; roll up in turban shape; fasten turbans with wooden picks. Stand up in buttered 10-by-6-by-2-inch baking dish; pour tomatoes into dish.
3. Bake 25 minutes, basting occasionally.
4. Remove picks; serve at once, garnished with ½ cup parsley. Makes 4 servings.

STUFFED FISH STEAK
(Pictured on page 26)

Butter or margarine
1 large onion, minced
½ cup snipped parsley
4 cups fresh white bread
   crumbs
½ pound fresh mushrooms,
   sliced
¼ cup lemon juice
Salt
Pepper

3 tablespoons milk
3 pounds swordfish,
   in 2 steaks,
   each ½ inch thick
Paprika
Cucumber, thinly sliced
Bottled oil-and-vinegar
   dressing
Lemon wedges

About 1 hour before serving:
1. In 2 tablespoons butter, in skillet, sauté onion until golden. Remove onion to large bowl; add parsley and bread crumbs.
2. In same skillet sauté mushrooms, with lemon juice, about 5 minutes. Add to crumb mixture, with 1 teaspoon salt, ¼ teaspoon pepper, and milk; toss together.
3. Start heating oven to 375°F.

Fish and French Fries

Stuffed Fish Steak

4. Sprinkle each side of steaks with salt, pepper, and paprika. Lay one steak with flat edge along 13-inch side of greased 13-by-9-by-2-inch baking dish. Pat bread-crumb mixture firmly on it; top with other steak. Dot with butter; sprinkle with paprika.
5. Bake fish 40 minutes, or until it flakes easily with fork.
6. Meanwhile, toss cucumber slices in some oil-and-vinegar dressing; refrigerate.
7. Serve fish right from baking dish, with drained cucumber slices and lemon wedges as pictured. Nice with a fruit cup, green beans with almonds, and rice pudding. Makes 8 servings.

SALMON SCALLOP DIVAN

1 10-ounce package frozen broccoli spears, thawed just enough to separate	1 1-pound 4-ounce can tomatoes, drained
3 tablespoons butter or margarine	½ cup grated process sharp-Cheddar cheese
3 tablespoons regular all-purpose flour	1½ cups day-old bread crumbs
½ teaspoon salt	1 1-pound can Chum salmon, in large chunks
⅛ teaspoon pepper	2 hard-cooked eggs, sliced lengthwise
2 cups reliquefied nonfat dry milk	

1. Start heating oven to 375°F.
2. Place broccoli in 2-quart casserole; then put in oven to bake while preparing rest of dish—about 10 minutes.
3. In saucepan melt butter; blend in flour, salt, and pepper, then milk. Cook, stirring, until thickened and smooth; remove from heat.
4. Carefully fold in tomatoes, cheese, and bread crumbs. Remove casserole from oven; arrange salmon over broccoli; pour on tomato mixture. Arrange egg slices on top, pressing them down into sauce.
5. Bake 25 minutes. Makes 4 servings.

SALMON BAKE

1 1-pound can salmon	1 tablespoon regular all-purpose flour
1 tablespoon lemon juice	
1 cup grated raw carrots	½ cup milk
1 small green pepper, diced	⅛ teaspoon pepper
	⅛ teaspoon paprika
½ cup mayonnaise or cooked salad dressing	1 egg, beaten
	2 slices white bread
Butter or margarine	Lemon slices or parsley sprigs (optional)

About 1 hour and 30 minutes before serving:
1. Start heating oven to 350°F.
2. Drain salmon well; remove backbone and skin; arrange in 1½-quart casserole, then sprinkle with lemon juice. Carefully fold in carrots, green pepper, and mayonnaise.
3. In small saucepan, over low heat, melt 1 tablespoon butter; stir in flour until smooth; then add milk, stirring until thickened. Remove from heat; stir in pepper, paprika, and egg; fold into salmon mixture.
4. Butter bread and cut into squares. Arrange, buttered-side up, over top of casserole.
5. Bake 25 to 30 minutes, or until bubbly-hot and golden.
6. Let cool about 5 minutes; then serve, garnished with lemon slices or parsley sprigs, if desired. Makes 4 servings.

TUNA AMANDINE

2 10-ounce packages frozen asparagus spears	2 6½- or 7-ounce cans tuna, flaked
1 package white-sauce mix	2 tablespoons melted butter or margarine
Slivered almonds	

About 1 hour before serving:
1. Start heating oven to 350°F.
2. Cook asparagus half the time package label directs; drain. Lay spears, side by side, in greased 10-by-6-by-2-inch baking dish.
3. Make up sauce mix as package label directs; fold in ¼ to ⅓ cup slivered almonds, and tuna; pour over asparagus.
4. Bake 30 minutes.
5. Unmold on heated platter. Sprinkle with melted butter and a few almonds. Serve with hot vichyssoise, celery-beet salad, refrigerated crescent rolls, and fruit and cheese for dessert. Makes 6 servings.
Note: If desired, prepare casserole early on day and refrigerate until 30 minutes before serving; then bake as in step 4.

COMPANY TUNA CASSEROLE

1 7¼-ounce package saltines (60)	1¼ cups milk
¾ cup melted butter or margarine	4 6½- or 7-ounce cans tuna, flaked
2 10½-ounce cans condensed cream-of-mushroom soup, undiluted	2 4-ounce cans pimento, drained, chopped
	12 lemon wedges
	Few parsley sprigs

About 1 hour before serving:
1. Crumble saltines into bowl; toss with melted butter. Into mushroom soup stir milk, then stir in tuna and pimento.
2. Start heating oven to 375°F.
3. In bottom of 2½- or 3-quart casserole spread one third of cracker mixture; cover with half of tuna mixture; repeat, then top with rest of crumbs.

4. Bake, uncovered, 40 minutes, or until hot.

5. Garnish with lemon wedges and parsley sprigs. Serve with beef bouillon, mixed vegetables, and lemon-chiffon pie. Makes 12 servings.

Note: If desired, prepare casserole early on day; refrigerate until about 1 hour before serving, then bake 50 minutes.

PANTRY TUNA SCALLOP

1 4½- or 5⅓-ounce package scalloped potatoes with seasonings	2 6½- or 7-ounce cans tuna, drained
1 cup thinly sliced onions	½ cup mayonnaise or cooked salad dressing
3 tablespoons butter or margarine	½ cup grated process Cheddar cheese
3 tablespoons regular all-purpose flour	½ teaspoon Tabasco
½ teaspoon salt	1 teaspoon prepared mustard
⅛ teaspoon pepper	Paprika
1¼ cups milk	

About 1 hour before serving:

1. In 2-quart casserole, prepare potatoes for baking as package label directs, adding onions. Bake at temperature indicated about 15 to 25 minutes, or until completely hot; remove from oven; stir with fork.

2. Meanwhile, in saucepan, over low heat, melt butter; stir in flour, salt, and pepper until well blended. Stir in milk gradually; cook, stirring, until thickened and smooth; fold in tuna.

3. Pour tuna mixture over potatoes. Spread with combined mayonnaise, cheese, Tabasco, and mustard. Return to oven.

4. Bake, uncovered, 10 to 15 minutes longer, or until hot and bubbly.

5. Let cool 10 minutes; sprinkle with paprika and serve. Makes 4 to 6 servings.

TUNA-CASHEW CASSEROLE

1 3-ounce can chow-mein noodles	¼ pound cashew nuts, salted or unsalted
1 10½-ounce can condensed cream-of-mushroom soup, undiluted	1 cup finely diced celery
	¼ cup minced onion
¼ cup water	Dash pepper
1 6½- or 7-ounce can tuna	Salt

About 1 hour before serving:

1. Start heating oven to 325°F.

2. Set aside ½ cup chow-mein noodles for garnish. In 1½-quart casserole combine rest of noodles with soup, water, tuna, cashew nuts, celery, onion, and pepper.

3. Taste mixture, then add salt if nuts were unsalted. Sprinkle reserved noodles over top.

4. Bake, uncovered, 40 minutes. Makes 5 servings.

ONE-DISH TUNA DINNER

14 small white onions	3 tablespoons regular all-purpose flour
1 teaspoon salt	
1 10-ounce package frozen peas	1⅔ cups milk
	1 6½- or 7-ounce can tuna, drained
3 tablespoons butter or margarine	1 cup packaged biscuit mix
	½ teaspoon sage

About 1 hour and 30 minutes before serving:

1. In medium saucepan, in boiling water to cover, cook onions with salt until almost tender. Add peas; cover and cook until both vegetables are tender—about 5 minutes longer. Drain, reserving liquid.

2. In 2-quart saucepan, melt butter; stir in flour, then gradually stir in 1 cup vegetable liquid and 1⅓ cups milk. Stir, over low heat, until thickened. Remove from heat; fold in onions and peas, then tuna in large pieces. Turn into 2-quart casserole.

3. Start heating oven to 450°F.

4. Combine biscuit mix with sage and ⅓ cup milk; on floured surface, knead about 8 to 10 times, then roll out into a square, ½ inch thick. Cut into 4 squares, or with large biscuit cutter, cut into 4 rounds. Place biscuits on top of onion-tuna mixture; brush biscuits lightly with milk.

5. Bake 20 minutes, or until golden.

6. Serve, spooning some of tuna mixture over each biscuit. Nice served with stuffed-olive coleslaw, grapefruit sections in grape juice, and tea or coffee. Makes 4 servings.

TOPSY-TURVY TUNA-LEMON PIE

1 unpeeled lemon, sliced	2 tablespoons lemon juice
1 6½- or 7-ounce can tuna (1 cup)	⅓ cup catchup
	1 egg, well beaten
2 tablespoons minced onion	¼ pound sliced process Cheddar cheese
1 tablespoon minced green pepper	
	6 tablespoons milk
¼ cup fresh bread crumbs	1 cup packaged biscuit mix
½ teaspoon dry mustard	

About 30 minutes before serving:

1. Start heating oven to 400°F.

2. Arrange lemon slices in bottom of greased 9-inch pie plate.

3. Mix tuna, onion, green pepper, bread crumbs, mustard, lemon juice, catchup, and egg. Spread over lemon slices; top with cheese slices.

4. With fork, stir milk into biscuit mix to make soft dough. Spread dough over cheese slices.

5. Bake, uncovered, 15 to 20 minutes, or until light-brown.

6. Loosen edges; quickly invert onto serving dish. Cut into wedges. Serve, hot, as is, or top with thin cream

sauce. Nice with buttered spinach with mushrooms, crisp radish roses, sherbet-topped melon wedges, and chocolate cookies. Makes 6 to 8 servings.

TUNA SUPPER CASSEROLE

1 10-ounce package frozen spinach, or 1 pound fresh spinach, washed	3 tablespoons butter or margarine
1 6½- or 7-ounce can tuna (1 cup)	1 tablespoon minced onion
1 3- or 4-ounce can sliced mushrooms	2 tablespoons regular all-purpose flour
2 tablespoons lemon juice	½ teaspoon salt
	⅛ teaspoon pepper
	1 bay leaf, crushed
	1 egg, slightly beaten

1. Start heating oven to 350°F.
2. If using frozen spinach, cook as package label directs; if fresh, cook in ½ inch boiling water 6 to 10 minutes, or until tender-crisp. Drain spinach well; season.
3. Drain excess oil from tuna. Drain mushrooms, reserving liquid. To mushroom liquid, add lemon juice, then enough water to measure 1 cup liquid.
4. In small saucepan melt 2 tablespoons butter; blend in minced onion, flour, salt, pepper, and bay leaf; then blend in mushroom liquid. Cook, stirring, until thick and smooth.
5. Beat sauce into egg; add mushrooms. Arrange spinach in 1½-quart casserole; top with tuna in big chunks; then top with sauce. Dot with 1 tablespoon butter.
6. Bake 30 minutes. Makes 4 servings.

SEA-STUFFED PEPPERS
(Pictured on page 17)

6 small green peppers	12 cooked, shelled, deveined shrimp (optional)
½ cup packaged dried bread crumbs	
¼ cup salad oil	1 teaspoon butter or margarine
1 cup shredded process Cheddar cheese	1 8-ounce can tomato sauce
1 6½- or 7-ounce can tuna, drained	1 teaspoon Worcestershire
2 tablespoons mayonnaise	¼ teaspoon orégano
2 tablespoons India relish	¼ teaspoon dill seeds
Salt	¼ teaspoon celery seeds
¼ teaspoon seasoned pepper	¼ teaspoon thyme
	Fresh dill sprigs

About 1 hour before serving:
1. Cut tops from peppers; seed them; cook, in boiling water, covered, 5 minutes; drain.
2. Start heating oven to 350°F.
3. Mix crumbs, salad oil, and cheese. Combine tuna, mayonnaise, relish, ¼ teaspoon salt, and seasoned pepper. Arrange green peppers in 2- or 2½-quart oval or oblong baking dish. In each pepper, layer crumb and tuna mixtures, ending with crumbs. Top each with 2 shrimp; dot with butter.
4. Combine tomato sauce with Worcestershire, ¼ teaspoon salt, orégano, dill seeds, celery seeds, and thyme. Pour ½ cup sauce into baking dish with peppers.
5. Bake 30 minutes.
6. Spoon remaining sauce over peppers; garnish with dill sprigs. Serve with green peas and onions, molded vegetable salad, poppy-seed rolls, and mocha cake. Makes 6 servings.

CRAB MEAT MARYLAND

¼ cup butter or margarine	1 pimento, minced
3 tablespoons regular all-purpose flour	Dash Tabasco
2 cups milk	2 tablespoons sherry
2 tablespoons minced onion	1 egg, beaten
½ teaspoon celery salt	1 teaspoon salt
⅛ teaspoon grated orange peel	Speck pepper
1 tablespoon snipped parsley	3 cups flaked fresh or thawed frozen or canned King-crab meat, drained
1 tablespoon minced green pepper	½ cup fresh bread crumbs
	1 tablespoon melted butter or margarine

1. Start heating oven to 350°F.
2. In double boiler melt ¼ cup butter; stir in flour and milk; cook, stirring, until thickened. Add onion, celery salt, orange peel, parsley, green pepper, pimento, and Tabasco. Remove from heat; add sherry.
3. Slowly stir some of sauce into egg, then stir egg mixture into rest of sauce. Add salt, pepper, and crab meat. Turn into greased 1½-quart casserole. Sprinkle with crumbs mixed with melted butter.
4. Bake, uncovered, 15 to 20 minutes, or until brown. Makes 6 servings.

FOR 2: Halve all ingredients; use 1-quart casserole.

To vary: Toss bread crumbs with ½ cup grated process sharp-Cheddar cheese; then sprinkle around edge of casserole. Bake 10 minutes, then arrange 3 half tomato slices down center of casserole and bake 5 minutes longer, or until golden.

CRAB MEAT IMPERIAL
(Pictured here)

Butter or margarine	1½ teaspoons dry mustard
2 tablespoons chopped green pepper	½ cup bottled capers, drained
2 tablespoons chopped pimento	1 tablespoon Worcestershire
9 tablespoons regular all-purpose flour	6 tablespoons mayonnaise
1½ teaspoons salt	3 pounds fresh lump crab meat, or 6 6-ounce
Pepper	packages frozen King-crab meat, or 6 6½-
Paprika	ounce cans King-crab meat
3 cups milk	
3 egg yolks, beaten	

About 1 hour before serving:
1. In 1 tablespoon butter, in small skillet, sauté green pepper and pimento 3 to 5 minutes.
2. In large saucepan melt 9 tablespoons butter; stir in flour, salt, speck pepper, and dash paprika until smooth. Slowly stir in milk; cook, stirring, until mixture becomes a smooth, thick sauce.
3. Start heating oven to 350°F.
4. To sauce, slowly add egg yolks, stirring constantly; then stir in mustard, capers, ⅛ teaspoon pepper, ⅛ teaspoon paprika, Worcestershire, 3 tablespoons may-onnaise, and green-pepper mixture. Blend well; fold in *well-drained* crab meat. Turn mixture into greased 2½-quart casserole; spread top with 3 tablespoons mayonnaise.
5. Bake about 30 minutes, or until golden on top. Makes about 12 servings.

CORN-SCALLOPED OYSTERS

¼ cup butter or margarine	1¼ cups coarsely-broken saltines
¼ cup light cream	½ cup grated process Cheddar cheese
½ teaspoon salt	
⅛ teaspoon pepper	2 dozen shucked oysters, drained (1 quart)*
½ teaspoon Worcestershire	1 12-ounce can whole-kernel corn, drained
2 tablespoons snipped parsley	

1. Start heating oven to 400°F.
2. In small saucepan combine butter, cream, salt, pepper, Worcestershire, and parsley; heat just long enough to melt butter.
3. Meanwhile, in greased 10-by-6-by-2-inch baking dish, arrange half of coarsely broken saltines.
4. Over saltines sprinkle cheese; on top arrange oysters and corn. Pour butter mixture over all; sprinkle with remaining saltines, crumbled.
5. Bake 20 to 25 minutes. Serve immediately. Makes 4 to 5 servings.
*With fingers, pick over oysters, to remove any bits of shell.

Spoon Bread, Crab Meat Imperial

Egg and/or Cheese Casseroles

SAVORY FILLED EGGS AND ASPARAGUS
(Pictured on page 2)

1 8-ounce package broad noodles	Seasoned salt
2 10-ounce packages frozen asparagus spears	Butter or margarine
	1 small onion, minced
Salt	¼ pound fresh mushrooms, sliced
6 extra-large hard-cooked eggs	1½ tablespoons regular all-purpose flour
Snipped chives	1¼ cups light cream
Mayonnaise	1¼ cups grated natural Swiss cheese
Prepared mustard	1 medium tomato, in 6 wedges
¼ teaspoon garlic powder	
¼ teaspoon seasoned pepper	

About 1 hour and 30 minutes before serving:

1. Cook noodles in 2 quarts boiling water 8 minutes; drain, rinse with cold water, then arrange in bottom of shallow, round 11-inch casserole, or 13-by-9-by-2 inch baking dish.
2. Cook asparagus in 2 cups boiling water with 1 teaspoon salt 5 minutes; drain, reserving 1½ cups asparagus liquid.
3. Cut ¾-inch slice from top of each egg; chop slices coarsely; set aside. Carefully scoop yolks from eggs; place yolks in small bowl; mash well with fork. Add 1 tablespoon snipped chives, ½ cup mayonnaise, 1 teaspoon prepared mustard, garlic powder, seasoned pepper, ¼ teaspoon seasoned salt, and ¼ teaspoon salt; mix until well blended.
4. Arrange scooped-out eggs over noodles in casserole.
5. Start heating oven to 350°F.
6. In medium saucepan melt 2 tablespoons butter; add minced onion and mushrooms; sauté lightly. Stir in flour, 2 tablespoons snipped chives, 1 teaspoon prepared mustard, ½ teaspoon seasoned salt, 1¼ teaspoons salt, and ¼ cup mayonnaise. Gradually stir in cream and reserved asparagus liquid. Bring to boil, then simmer a few minutes; now stir in Swiss cheese and chopped egg slices. Stir until cheese melts and is smooth; pour over noodles and around eggs.
7. With hard-cooked egg-yolk mixture in decorating bag with large pastry tube number 7 in place, fill each scooped-out egg. Next arrange asparagus spears around

eggs, overlapping slightly. Dot them with 2 tablespoons butter.
8. Bake 10 minutes, then increase oven heat to 400°F. and bake 10 minutes longer, or until egg tops are golden.
9. Remove from oven; place a tomato wedge between every two eggs, then serve. Makes 6 servings.

EGGS DIVAN

Deviled Eggs:	**Broccoli and Sauce:**
6 hard-cooked eggs	1 package frozen broccoli
1 2¼-ounce can deviled ham	1½ tablespoons butter or margarine
¼ teaspoon Worcestershire	1½ tablespoons regular all-purpose flour
½ teaspoon grated onion	⅛ teaspoon dry mustard
½ teaspoon salt	½ teaspoon salt
½ teaspoon dry mustard	Dash pepper
Dash pepper	¾ cup milk
1 to 2 tablespoons light cream	½ cup grated process sharp-Cheddar cheese

1. Prepare Deviled Eggs: Cut ¼-inch slice from one end of each shelled egg; carefully remove yolk. Mash yolks and end slices; add ham, Worcestershire, onion, salt, mustard, pepper, and cream. Mix well; then use to fill egg whites.
2. Cook broccoli as package label directs.
3. Start heating oven to 400°F.
4. In saucepan, make sauce: Melt butter; stir in flour, mustard, salt, and pepper, then milk; cook until thickened. Add cheese; stir until smooth.
5. Arrange broccoli in 10-by-6-by-2-inch baking dish; stand eggs, with stuffed ends up, between and on broccoli pieces. Pour sauce over all.
6. Bake, uncovered, 40 minutes, or until bubbly. Makes 4 or 5 servings.

BROCCOLI-AND-EGG CASSEROLE

2 tablespoons butter or margarine	¼ teaspoon salt
	⅛ teaspoon pepper
2 tablespoons minced onion	¼ teaspoon garlic salt
4 large mushrooms, thinly sliced	6 eggs, unbeaten
	½ teaspoon salt
1 10-ounce package frozen chopped broccoli, partially thawed	⅛ teaspoon pepper
	½ cup grated process Cheddar cheese

1. Start heating oven to 350°F.
2. In butter, in skillet, sauté onion and mushrooms until golden. Arrange broccoli on top. Sprinkle with ¼ teaspoon salt, ⅛ teaspoon pepper, and garlic salt. Simmer, covered, 5 minutes; drain.
3. With fork, blend eggs, ½ teaspoon salt, and ⅛ teaspoon pepper until just mixed; stir in cheese.

4. Turn broccoli mixture into greased 1½-quart casserole; pour egg mixture over broccoli. Set casserole in shallow baking pan; place in oven, then pour ¼ inch boiling water into pan.

5. Bake 20 to 25 minutes, or until a silver knife, inserted in center, comes out clean. Serve at once. Makes 4 servings.

BAKED EGGS EN CASSEROLE

¼ cup butter or margarine	1 cup drained cooked or canned peas
3 cooked medium potatoes, in large cubes	1 pimento, slivered (optional)
½ pound Bologna, in ½-inch cubes	2 tomatoes, slivered
Salt	2 tablespoons snipped parsley
Pepper	4 eggs
	2 tablespoons light cream

About 30 minutes before serving:
1. Start heating oven to 425°F.
2. In butter, in skillet, sauté potatoes until lightly browned. Add Bologna, 1 teaspoon salt, ¼ teaspoon pepper, peas, and pimento; cook 3 minutes. Add tomatoes and parsley; cook until hot.
3. Turn Bologna mixture into 1½-quart baking dish. Make 4 depressions in top; in each break an egg; sprinkle eggs with salt and pepper.
4. Bake 10 minutes, or until of desired doneness; pour on cream.
5. Serve with toasty bread, hearts of lettuce with lemon French dressing, sliced bananas topped with canned crushed pineapple. Makes 4 servings.

ZUCCHINI-CHIP OMELET

3 tablespoons butter or margarine	¼ teaspoon pepper
1 medium onion, thinly sliced	2 eggs, unbeaten
1 clove garlic	½ cup milk
2 pounds zucchini, coarsely grated	⅓ cup grated Parmesan cheese
1½ teaspoons salt	½ cup coarsely-crushed potato chips
	Paprika

About 35 minutes before serving:
1. Start heating oven to 350°F.
2. In butter, in large skillet or chicken fryer, sauté onion slices and garlic until golden. Remove garlic; add zucchini, salt, and pepper; cook, covered, 5 to 7 minutes, or until zucchini is fork-tender.
3. Meanwhile, beat eggs with milk and cheese. In 1½-quart shallow casserole, combine zucchini and egg mixtures. Sprinkle with potato chips and paprika.
4. Bake about 20 minutes, or until firm and set. Serve at once. Makes 6 generous servings.

EGGS IN RICE NESTS

2 cups cooked rice	1½ tablespoons melted butter or margarine
1 10-ounce package frozen mixed vegetables	¼ teaspoon salt
½ cup grated process Cheddar cheese	⅛ teaspoon pepper
	3 eggs

1. Cook rice and mixed vegetables as package labels direct; drain.
2. Start heating oven to 400°F.
3. Combine rice, vegetables, cheese, butter, salt, and pepper. Pour into 1-quart casserole. With spoon, make 3 small wells in rice mixture; into them break eggs.
4. Bake, covered, about 15 minutes, or until of desired doneness. Makes 3 servings.

FOR 6: Double all ingredients; make as above, using 2-quart casserole and baking for about 20 minutes.

SPICY EGGS 'N' HAM

3 tablespoons butter or margarine	1 tablespoon Worcestershire
3 tablespoons regular all-purpose flour	1 tablespoon chili sauce
1 teaspoon dry mustard	Dash Tabasco
¾ teaspoon salt	6 hard-cooked eggs, sliced
⅛ teaspoon pepper	2 cups diced, cooked ham
1½ cups milk	½ cup cut-up ripe olives
1 teaspoon prepared horse-radish	¾ cup diced process sharp-Cheddar cheese

1. Start heating oven to 400°F.
2. In saucepan melt butter; stir in flour, mustard, salt, and pepper, then milk; cook, stirring, until thickened. Stir in horse-radish, Worcestershire, chili sauce, and Tabasco.
3. In 1½-quart casserole, arrange layers of eggs, ham, olives, cheese, and sauce.
4. Bake 25 to 30 minutes. Makes 4 or 5 servings.

CHEESE STRATA

12 day-old bread slices	½ teaspoon dry or prepared mustard
½ pound thinly-sliced process Cheddar cheese	1 tablespoon minced onion
4 eggs, unbeaten	1 teaspoon salt
2½ cups milk	⅛ teaspoon pepper

1. Remove crusts from bread. Arrange 6 bread slices in greased 12-by-8-by-2-inch baking dish; cover with cheese slices, then with rest of bread slices.
2. In large bowl beat eggs; blend in milk, mustard, onion, salt, and pepper; pour over bread. Refrigerate 1 hour.
3. Meanwhile, start heating oven to 325°F.
4. Bake strata 50 minutes, or until puffy and brown.
5. Serve at once, with broccoli spears with lemon

butter, marinated tomato wedges on lettuce, and canned peach halves sprinkled with coconut. Makes 6 servings.

FOR 2: Halve ingredients; use 10-by-6-by-2 inch baking dish; bake as above.

CHEESE PUDDING: Omit mustard and onion. Serve with jelly.

CORN-CHEESE BAKE: Spread 1½ cups cooked, frozen, or canned whole-kernel corn on top of cheese. Bake 1 hour.

L.B.'S BAKED SANDWICHES: Blend ½ pound process pimento cheese, grated, with 1 cup sliced ripe olives, 1 4½-ounce can deviled ham, ¼ cup minced onion, ½ cup minced celery, 2 tablespoons catchup, 1 teaspoon salt, and ¼ cup mayonnaise. Spread this mixture over 6 bread slices in baking dish; cover with remaining bread slices. Pour on egg and milk mixture; refrigerate 1 hour. Then bake 45 minutes. To serve, cut around each sandwich and lift to heated platter.

NAN'S FRENCH FONDUE

1½ long loaves French bread
½ cup butter or margarine
½ cup sharp prepared mustard
1½ pounds natural or process sharp-Cheddar cheese, sliced ¼ inch thick
4 eggs, well beaten
5 cups hot milk
1½ teaspoons Worcestershire
1 teaspoon salt
⅛ teaspoon cayenne pepper
¼ teaspoon paprika

Day before:
1. Slice French bread into ½-inch slices; spread generously with butter and mustard.
2. In 4-quart casserole, alternate layers of bread and cheese slices to fill casserole.
3. Combine eggs, milk, Worcestershire, salt, and cayenne. Pour over bread and cheese layers. Sprinkle top with paprika. Refrigerate, covered, overnight.

About 1 hour and 45 minutes before serving:
1. Start heating oven to 350°F.
2. Remove fondue from refrigerator.
3. Bake, uncovered, 1½ hours. Makes 8 servings.

FOR 4: Use ¾ of long loaf of French bread. Reduce milk to 2 cups, rest of ingredients to half. Bake in 2-quart casserole 1 hour.

CHICKEN-CHEESE FONDUE

4 egg whites
4 egg yolks
2 cups small fresh bread cubes
1 cup grated process sharp-Cheddar cheese
1 10½-ounce can condensed cream-of-chicken soup, undiluted

1. Start heating oven to 325°F.
2. In medium bowl, with mixer or hand beater, beat egg whites until stiff but not dry.
3. With same beater, beat egg yolks until thick and lemon-colored; add bread cubes, cheese, and soup; mix well. Fold gently into egg whites; turn into greased 1½-quart casserole.
4. Bake 1 hour, or until silver knife, inserted in center, comes out clean.
5. Serve at once. Makes 6 servings.

INDIVIDUAL CHEESE CASSEROLES

6 slices toast, cubed
1 8-ounce package process sharp-Cheddar cheese, shredded
¾ cup sliced stuffed olives
4 eggs, unbeaten
3 cups milk
1 teaspoon salt
¼ teaspoon pepper
1 teaspoon prepared mustard

About 1 hour before serving:
1. Divide half of toast cubes between 6 1-cup individual casseroles. Top each with layer of half of shredded cheese, then half of sliced olives. Repeat layers.
2. Start heating oven to 350°F.
3. Beat eggs with milk, salt, pepper, and mustard. Pour an equal amount of egg mixture into each casserole.
4. Bake 40 minutes, or until puffed up and browned. Makes 6 servings.

SWISS SURPRISE CASSEROLES

¾ cup diced cooked ham
1½ cups grated natural Swiss cheese
3 eggs, unbeaten
1 cup milk
½ teaspoon salt
⅛ teaspoon pepper
⅛ teaspoon onion salt
1 10-ounce package corn-bread mix

1. Start heating oven to 425°F.
2. In 2 individual 1½-cup casseroles layer ham and Swiss cheese.
3. With hand beater, beat together eggs, milk, salt, pepper, and onion salt; pour over ham and cheese in each casserole.
4. Prepare corn-bread mix as package label directs; with spatula, spread ¼ cup batter over top of egg-cheese

mixture in each casserole. (Use rest of corn-bread mixture to make 4 muffins; bake as directed on package label. Next day, serve toasted at breakfast.)

5. Bake casserole 20 minutes, or until golden. Makes 2 servings.

VEGETABLE-CHEESE BAKE

4 eggs, separated
1 cup milk
3 slices white bread, crusts
   removed
¾ teaspoon salt
½ teaspoon dry mustard
¼ teaspoon monosodium glutamate
⅛ teaspoon pepper
1 cup cottage cheese

2 cups finely-chopped, cooked
   vegetables
1 small onion, minced
2 tablespoons minced green pepper
   or snipped parsley
1 10½-ounce can condensed
   tomato soup, undiluted
2 tablespoons butter or margarine

Day before:
In mixing bowl, beat egg yolks with fork. Add milk, bread, salt, mustard, monosodium glutamate, and pepper. Let bread soften; break up with fork; add cottage cheese, vegetables, onion, and green pepper. Refrigerate overnight.

About 1 hour before serving:
1. Start heating oven to 350°F.
2. Beat egg whites until stiff; fold into cheese mixture. Pour into well-greased 10-by-6-by-2-inch or 8-by-8-by-2-inch baking dish.
3. Bake 45 minutes, or until firm.
4. Cut into squares. Heat soup with butter; serve as sauce over squares. Makes 4 servings.

Soufflés suffer from drafts and standing, so when you prepare one be certain of your timing. Plan to serve a soufflé at once, *but if it must stand (not more than 10 minutes), turn oven to 250° F. and don't peek!*

BACON-CHEESE CROWN
(Pictured here)

½ cup butter or margarine
1 cup regular all-purpose flour
2½ teaspoons salt
¼ teaspoon pepper
⅛ teaspoon nutmeg
2 cups milk
½ cup heavy cream

2 cups grated natural Swiss cheese
½ cup snipped chives
8 eggs, separated
About 9 slices white bread
6 lean bacon slices
1 small mushroom

About 2 hours and 30 minutes before serving:
1. In large saucepan melt butter; stir in flour, salt, pepper, and nutmeg. Slowly stir in milk and cream, blending well. Cook, stirring constantly, until smooth and thickened. Blend in grated cheese (reserve 2 tablespoons) and chives.
2. Remove from heat, turn into large bowl, then stir in egg yolks, one at a time. Let cool slightly.
3. Start heating oven to 350°F.
4. Butter a china soufflé dish which measures 10 cups to brim. Line

Bacon-Cheese Crown

bottom of dish with about 3 bread slices, cut to fit. Now cut 6 bread slices in half lengthwise. Place them upright, side by side, in circle around inner edge of dish. Lace a strip of bacon, in figure-eight fashion, around every two slices.

5. Fold a 35-inch length of foil, 12 inches wide, in half lengthwise; wrap around outside of dish so that a collar 3 inches high stands above rim; fasten with cellophane tape.

6. In large bowl, beat egg whites until stiff; carefully fold into cooled cheese mixture; pour into soufflé dish. Cut mushroom into thin slices; lay some in a circle and one on top of soufflé mixture as pictured; sprinkle with reserved cheese.

7. Bake 1 hour and 40 minutes, or until golden.

8. Carefully remove foil collar. Serve at once. Makes 8 servings.

MUSHROOM-CHEESE SOUFFLÉ

2 eggs, separated	Dash pepper
2 tablespoons milk	1 cup cottage cheese
3 tablespoons regular all-purpose flour	2 tablespoons minced onion
½ teaspoon salt	1 3- or 4-ounce can sliced mushrooms, drained

1. Start heating oven to 300°F.
2. With hand beater, beat egg yolks until light and foamy.
3. Stir milk gradually into flour; add to egg yolks; beat well. Add salt, pepper, and cottage cheese; beat until blended.
4. Beat egg whites until stiff. Gently fold into egg yolk mixture with onion and mushrooms. Turn into greased 1-quart casserole.
5. Bake about 50 minutes, or until golden brown on top. Makes 2 servings.

Note: Or bake in 2 greased 2-cup casseroles for 45 minutes.

CORN SOUFFLÉ

¼ cup milk	Dash pepper
½ cup grated natural sharp-Cheddar cheese	1 12-ounce can vacuum-packed whole-kernel corn, drained
½ cup mayonnaise	
¼ cup regular all-purpose flour	2 tablespoons snipped parsley
¼ teaspoon onion salt	4 egg whites

1. Start heating oven to 325°F.
2. In small saucepan heat milk with cheese until cheese melts.
2. In small bowl, with spoon, mix mayonnaise, flour, onion salt, and pepper; slowly stir in milk mixture; blend well. Stir in corn and parsley.
4. In large bowl, with mixer or hand beater, beat egg

whites until stiff. With spoon, gently fold corn mixture into egg whites until blended. Pour into oiled 1-quart casserole.

5. Bake, uncovered, 50 minutes, or until silver knife, inserted in center, comes out clean.

6. Serve at once, as vegetable. Or if used as main dish serve with heated cheese sauce (from a jar), or use canned Cheddar-cheese soup. Makes 4 servings.

SWEET-POTATO SOUFFLÉ

2 cups mashed cooked sweet potatoes*	¼ teaspoon allspice
¾ cup hot milk	¼ teaspoon cardamom
3 tablespoons butter or margarine	1 tablespoon grated orange peel
¼ teaspoon salt	2 egg yolks
	2 egg whites

1. Start heating oven to 325°F.
2. Combine potatoes with milk, butter, salt, allspice, cardamom, and orange peel.
3. Beat egg yolks well; add to potato mixture.
4. In medium bowl, beat egg whites until stiff; carefully fold potato mixture into whites. Turn into greased 1-quart casserole.
5. Bake, uncovered, 1 hour and 30 minutes. Makes 6 servings.

*You may use canned sweet potatoes.

CHEESE AND TUNA SOUFFLÉ

1¾ cups undiluted evaporated milk	½ teaspoon monosodium glutamate
4 tablespoons regular all-purpose flour	½ pound process sharp-Cheddar cheese
½ teaspoon salt	4 eggs, separated
¼ teaspoon dry mustard	¾ cup flaked canned tuna
¼ teaspoon Tabasco	

1. Start heating oven to 300°F.
2. Into top of double boiler pour evaporated milk. Add flour, salt, mustard, Tabasco, and monosodium glutamate; with hand beater, beat until smooth. Place over boiling water and beat until slightly thickened—about 5 minutes.
3. Slice cheese into milk mixture, then blend occasionally with hand beater, until thickened and cheese has melted — about 10 minutes. Beat until smooth; remove from heat.
4. Add egg yolks, one at a time, beating after each addition. (Now wash beater thoroughly; any trace of cheese mixture will prevent egg whites from whipping.) Fold in tuna. In ungreased 2-quart casserole beat egg whites until very stiff but not dry; gradually fold in cheese mixture.
5. Bake 1 hour. Serve immediately. Makes 4 servings.

To vary: Use finely chopped chicken for tuna.

CHEESE PUFF WITH VEGETABLES, HAM, AND MUSHROOMS

1 10-ounce package frozen
   cauliflower
1 10-ounce package frozen
   peas
Butter or margarine
½ pound fresh mushrooms,
   quartered
5 eggs, separated

½ cup commercial sour
   cream
¾ teaspoon salt
⅛ teaspoon pepper
⅛ teaspoon nutmeg
¼ cup regular all-purpose
   flour
Grated Parmesan cheese
¼ pound cooked ham, diced

About 1 hour and 30 minutes before serving:
1.   Cook cauliflower with peas as package labels direct; drain; set aside. In 1 to 2 tablespoons butter, in skillet, sauté mushrooms until golden; set aside.

2.   Beat ⅓ cup butter until creamy; beat in egg yolks, one at a time; beat in sour cream, salt, pepper, and nutmeg. Gradually beat in flour and 2 tablespoons grated Parmesan cheese.
3.   Start heating oven to 350°F.
4.   Beat egg whites until stiff; fold in sour-cream mixture until smooth. Spread half of soufflé mixture in bottom of buttered 10-by-6-by-2-inch baking dish. Top with half of cauliflower, peas, mushrooms, and ham; sprinkle with 3 tablespoons cheese. Pour on rest of soufflé mixture.
5.   Arrange rest of vegetables and ham down center of dish; sprinkle with 3 tablespoons cheese; dot with 1 tablespoon butter.
6.   Bake 35 minutes, or until golden.
7.   Serve at once. Makes 4 servings.

A Bonus Recipe

Roll up fine flavor in Crêpes Lasagne and soon you'll be getting requests not only from the family, but from guests as well. It might even turn out to be one of those recipes that become a specialty of the house! And the advantage is that the crêpes themselves can be made up to a month ahead, frozen, and thawed on the day of your dinner. Then make the sauce and be prepared for compliments.

CRÊPES LASAGNE

3 cups milk
3 eggs
2 tablespoons melted
   butter or margarine
Salt
2¼ cups sifted regular all-
   purpose flour
2 8-ounce cans tomato
   sauce
2 10¼-ounce cans meat
   sauce for spaghetti
1½ teaspoons orégano
1 teaspoon monosodium
   glutamate
¼ teaspoon seasoned
   pepper

½ teaspoon basil leaves,
   crushed
1 pound sweet Italian
   sausage
2 cups ricotta cheese
12 packaged Mozzarella
   cheese slices
1 cup shredded Parmesan
   cheese
Snipped parsley (optional)
Fresh tomato slices, halved
   (optional)
Pitted ripe olives
   (optional)

Make any time up to 1 month ahead, then freeze:
1.   In large bowl combine milk, eggs, melted butter, 1½ teaspoons salt, and flour; with hand beater, beat until smooth.
2.   Into greased 10-inch aluminum skillet pour ⅓ cup batter; tilt to coat bottom of skillet evenly. Cook, over medium heat, turning once, until light brown on both sides. Place on wax paper. Repeat, each time removing skillet from heat before pouring in batter, and stacking crêpes between pieces of wax paper as you go. Now freezer-wrap, freeze crêpes.

About 2 hours and 30 minutes before serving:
1.   Remove crêpes from freezer; let stand until thawed enough to separate.
2.   Meanwhile, combine tomato sauce, meat sauce, ½ teaspoon salt, orégano, monosodium glutamate, seasoned pepper, and basil; bring to boil, then simmer, uncovered, over low heat, 30 minutes.
3.   Meanwhile, in skillet sauté sausage until done; cut into ¼-inch slices.
4.   Start heating oven to 350°F.
5.   On one crêpe, spread 1 rounded tablespoon ricotta cheese; top with 1 slice Mozzarella, then sprinkle with about 6 or 7 sausage slices. Roll up, jelly-roll fashion, and place, seam side down, in 4-quart round casserole measuring 12 by 2½ inches, or in a 13-by-9-by-2-inch baking dish. Repeat with rest of crêpes, placing 4 or 5 crêpes, about 2 inches apart, on top of first layer, so all fit. Pour sauce over filled crêpes; cover casserole with foil.
6.   Bake 45 minutes; remove foil and sprinkle crêpes with Parmesan cheese. Bake 15 minutes longer, or until cheese is golden.
7.   If desired, just before serving, garnish top of casserole with snipped parsley, tomato slices, and ripe olives. Makes 12 servings.

FOR 6: Make as directed above, but use 1 egg plus 1 egg white and half of all other ingredients. Bake, in 8-by-8-by-2-inch oven-glass baking dish, 35 minutes, then top with Parmesan cheese; bake 15 minutes.

Noodle, Rice, and Pasta Casseroles

FAR-EASTERN CASSEROLES

2 cups medium noodles
1 12-ounce can luncheon meat, in large cubes
1 9-ounce package frozen cut green beans, cooked, or 1 16-ounce can green beans, drained

1 envelope golden gravy or sauce mix (to make 1¼ cups)
1 cup shredded process Cheddar cheese
2 tablespoons catchup
1 tablespoon prepared horse-radish

About 1 hour and 30 minutes before serving:
1. Start heating oven to 350°F.
2. Cook noodles as package label directs; drain.
3. In large bowl combine luncheon meat and drained green beans.
4. Prepare gravy mix as package label directs, then stir in cheese, catchup, and horse-radish. Add, with noodles, to meat. Pour into 1½-quart casserole.
5. Bake, covered, 40 to 45 minutes, or until very hot. Makes 4 servings.

HINGHAM GOULASH

1 8-ounce package flat ¼-inch noodles
6 bacon slices, in small pieces
1 large onion, chopped
1 pound chuck, ground
1 3-ounce jar stuffed olives, sliced
1½ 10¾-ounce cans condensed tomato soup, undiluted
½ soup-can water

1 10½-ounce can condensed consommé, undiluted
½ teaspoon salt
⅛ teaspoon pepper
½ teaspoon granulated sugar
1½ teaspoons bottled thick meat sauce
½ teaspoon orégano
½ teaspoon thyme
1 cup grated Cheddar cheese

About 2 hours and 15 minutes before serving:
1. Start heating oven to 300°F.
2. Cook noodles as package label directs; drain.
3. Meanwhile, in skillet, cook bacon until crisp; remove bacon from skillet.
4. In bacon drippings, brown onion; then add chuck and quickly brown it. Stir in olives, tomato soup, water, consommé, salt, pepper, sugar, meat sauce, orégano, and thyme; heat.

5. Arrange noodles in buttered 2½-quart casserole. Pour on sauce; top with bacon and toss well, then sprinkle cheese over all.
6. Bake, covered, 1 hour; then uncover and bake 30 minutes longer.
7. Remove from oven and let casserole stand 15 minutes before serving. Serve buffet style. Nice with tossed mixed vegetable salad, garlic bread, raspberry-sherbet and vanilla-ice cream balls, ginger cookies, and coffee. Makes 6 servings.

MARTHA'S COMPANY CASSEROLE

4 cups medium noodles (½ pound)
1 tablespoon butter or margarine
1 pound chuck, ground
2 8-ounce cans tomato sauce
1 cup cottage cheese (½ pound)

1 8-ounce package soft cream cheese
¼ cup commercial sour cream
⅓ cup snipped scallions
1 tablespoon minced green pepper
2 tablespoons melted butter or margarine

Early on day:
1. Cook noodles as package label directs; drain.
2. Meanwhile, in 1 tablespoon hot butter in skillet, sauté chuck until browned. Stir in tomato sauce. Remove from heat.
3. Combine cottage cheese, cream cheese, sour cream, scallions, and green pepper.
4. In 2-quart casserole spread half of noodles. Cover with cheese mixture, then cover with rest of noodles. Pour on melted butter, then meat mixture. Refrigerate.
About 1 hour before serving:
1. Start heating oven to 375°F.
2. Bake casserole 45 minutes, or until heated through. Makes 6 servings.
FOR 2: Halve all ingredients; use 1-quart casserole.

LASAGNA VITE
(Pictured opposite)

1½ 8-ounce packages wide noodles
Salad oil
1½ pounds chuck, ground
1½ teaspoons salt
¼ teaspoon pepper
2 cups favorite spaghetti sauce

1 pound creamed cottage cheese
¼ cup commercial sour cream
1½ 8-ounce packages pizza-cheese slices*

Day before, or early on day:
1. Cook noodles as package label directs; drain, then toss with 2 tablespoons salad oil until well coated.
2. In skillet, brown chuck, then drain very well; add salt, pepper, and spaghetti sauce; stir well.
3. Combine cottage cheese with sour cream.

Lasagna Vite

4.   Arrange half of noodles in 12-by-8-by-2-inch baking dish; cover with half of meat-sauce mixture, next a layer of cheese slices (using 1 package), then all of cottage-cheese mixture. Top with remaining noodles, then rest of cheese, in ½-inch strips, laid "lattice-fashion" across top as pictured on page 39. Then spoon rest of meat-sauce mixture into lattice spaces. Cover tightly with saran or foil; refrigerate.

About 30 minutes before serving:
1.   Start heating oven to 350°F.
2.   Brush surface of cheese strips with salad oil.
3.   Bake 30 minutes, or until cheese melts and is golden.
4.   Serve with salad of crisp lettuce and raw vegetables, chunks of Italian bread, and a bowl of fruit or lemon sherbet. Makes 6 servings.
*You may substitute 1½ 8-ounce packages Mozzarella, thinly sliced, for pizza cheese.

KRAUT-NOODLE CASSEROLE

2 cups medium-wide
  noodles (4 ounces)
2 tablespoons butter or
  margarine

1 1-pound 4-ounce can
  sauerkraut, drained
  (2½ cups)
Pepper
¼ pound packaged process
  Cheddar-cheese slices

1.   Start heating oven to 300°F.
2.   Cook noodles as package label directs until barely tender; drain. Add butter; toss until well mixed.
3.   Spread three fourths of sauerkraut in 1½-quart casserole or 10-by-6-by-2-inch baking dish. Sprinkle with pepper. Top with noodles, cheese slices, and rest of sauerkraut.
4.   Bake, covered, 1 hour. Makes 4 or 5 servings.
FOR 2: Halve ingredients, using 1 1-pound can sauerkraut.
Note: Leftovers may be reheated.

MAZETTI

¾ cup finely-chopped celery
¼ cup melted butter or
  margarine
1 cup minced onion
¾ cup minced green
  pepper
1 pound chuck, ground
1 pound pork, ground
1½ teaspoons salt
½ teaspoon pepper

1½ 8-ounce packages
  wide noodles
¼ cup butter or margarine
1 3- or 4-ounce can
  sliced mushrooms,
  undrained
2 10¾-ounce cans
  condensed tomato soup,
  undiluted
Grated Parmesan cheese

Day before, or early on day:
1.   In saucepan, in water to cover, cook celery until tender; drain; set aside.
2.   In large skillet, in melted butter, sauté onion and

green pepper 5 minutes; stir in ground chuck and pork, salt, and pepper; cook, uncovered, until meat loses its red color.
3.   Cook noodles as package label directs; drain; rinse. Turn into 3-quart casserole; toss with ¼ cup butter; stir in meat mixture, celery, mushrooms, and soup; toss to mix well. Sprinkle with Parmesan cheese; cover; refrigerate.

About 1 hour and 20 minutes before serving:
1.   Start heating oven to 400°F.
2.   Bake casserole, uncovered, 1 hour and 15 minutes, or until hot in center. Makes 12 servings.

THOR'S COMPANY CASSEROLE

2 tablespoons salad oil
1 clove garlic
1 pound veal round (thin
  slice cut into pieces)
Salt
Pepper
2 3- or 4-ounce cans sliced
  mushrooms
4 ounces medium noodles

½ cup commercial sour
  cream
¼ pound Swiss cheese,
  sliced
2 tomatoes, sliced
½ cup dry white wine
½ cup grated Parmesan
  cheese

1.   Start heating oven to 400°F.
2.   In hot oil in skillet, brown garlic with veal, sprinkling veal with ½ teaspoon salt and ⅛ teaspoon pepper. Remove garlic.
3.   Add undrained mushrooms. Simmer, covered, 15 to 20 minutes. Meanwhile, cook noodles as package label directs; drain; toss with sour cream.
4.   In 1½-quart casserole place half of noodle mixture, half of veal and mushrooms, then half of Swiss cheese and tomato slices. Sprinkle with ½ teaspoon salt and ⅛ teaspoon pepper. Repeat layers. Into gravy in skillet stir wine and Parmesan cheese. Pour this mixture over casserole.
5.   Bake, uncovered, about 25 minutes. Makes 6 servings.

PILAF ORIENTAL

½ cup butter or margarine
2 cups uncooked regular
  or processed white rice
1 1-pint 2-ounce can
  tomato juice

1 13¾-ounce can chicken
  broth (1¾ cups)
½ teaspoon salt
Snipped parsley

About 1 hour before serving:
1.   Start heating oven to 375°F.
2.   In butter, in Dutch oven, sauté rice until it is brown and almost all of butter is absorbed, stirring frequently to prevent scorching.
3.   While stirring, slowly add tomato juice, chicken broth, and salt. Pour into 2½-quart casserole.
4.   Bake, covered, 45 minutes, or until rice is tender.

5. Uncover immediately; fluff up rice with fork and sprinkle with parsley; serve. Makes 8 servings.

GREEN-AND-GOLD CASSEROLE

2 cups milk
2 cups grated Cheddar
  cheese
2 cups cooked rice
1 cup snipped parsley

½ clove garlic, minced
2 eggs, slightly beaten
1 10½-ounce can con-
  densed cream-of-mush-
  room soup, undiluted

1. Start heating oven to 350°F.
2. Heat milk with cheese until cheese is partially melted. Add rice, parsley, garlic, eggs, and soup; mix well. Pour into 2-quart casserole. Place casserole in large baking pan; set on oven rack. Fill pan half full of hot water.
3. Bake casserole, uncovered, 1 hour and 20 minutes, or until mixture is browned and set. Serve at once. Makes 6 servings.

RANCHERO

1 pound chuck, ground
1 tablespoon salad oil
1 clove garlic, minced
1 teaspoon salt
¾ cup uncooked packaged
  precooked white rice
1 large onion, minced
½ cup chopped green
  pepper

1 teaspoon chili powder
1 1-pound can tomatoes
1 16- or 17-ounce can
  kidney beans
¼ pound Cheddar cheese,
  sliced
4 ripe olives, sliced

1. Start heating oven to 350°F.
2. Meanwhile, in large bowl combine chuck, salad oil, garlic, salt, rice, onion, green pepper, chili powder, tomatoes, and beans; mix well. Pour into greased 2-quart casserole.
3. Bake 50 minutes. Then top with sliced cheese and olive slices; bake 5 minutes longer, or until cheese is melted.
4. Serve with crisp raw relishes—celery, carrots, olives, pickles — and crunchy hard rolls, with pecan pie for dessert. Makes 8 servings.

ITALIAN RICE WITH EGGPLANT

Olive or salad oil
1 large eggplant, pared,
  thinly sliced
1 tablespoon butter or
  margarine
1 thin slice salt pork, diced
1 medium onion, minced
1 6-ounce can tomato paste
2 8-ounce cans tomato
  sauce
1 cup water

1 teaspoon salt
¼ teaspoon pepper
4 cups chicken broth
1½ cups uncooked
  regular white rice
¼ cup butter or margarine
¼ pound Mozzarella
  cheese, thinly sliced
¼ cup grated Parmesan
  cheese
1 teaspoon basil

1. In a little hot oil in Dutch oven, sauté eggplant slices on both sides until golden; remove eggplant.
2. In same Dutch oven, heat 1 tablespoon oil and 1 tablespoon butter. In it, sauté salt pork and onion until salt pork is crisp and browned. Now add tomato paste, tomato sauce, water, salt, and pepper; simmer, covered, 40 minutes.
3. Add chicken broth and rice. Bring to boil, then simmer, covered, 45 minutes, stirring occasionally. Stir in ¼ cup butter.
4. Start heating oven to 400°F.
5. In greased 3-quart casserole arrange half of rice, half of eggplant, then half of Mozzarella. Repeat. Sprinkle with Parmesan cheese and basil.
6. Bake, uncovered, 25 minutes. Makes 6 servings.

POLYNESIAN RICE MINGLE

1 cup uncooked packaged
  wild rice
1 cup uncooked regular
  white rice
3 tablespoons minced
  onion
3 tablespoons soy sauce

4 chicken-bouillon cubes
4 cups boiling water
1½ cups Macadamia nuts,
  coarsely chopped
  (optional)
¼ cup snipped parsley
  (optional)

Day before:
1. Start heating oven to 350°F.
2. In 2-quart casserole combine wild rice, white rice, onion, and soy sauce.
3. Dissolve bouillon cubes in boiling water; stir into rice mixture in casserole.
4. Bake rice, covered, 45 minutes. Cool a little; refrigerate.
About 20 minutes before serving:
1. Start heating oven to 350°F.
2. Remove casserole from refrigerator; bake 15 minutes, or until hot.
3. Just before serving, sprinkle rice with Macadamia nuts and snipped parsley, if desired. Makes 4 to 6 servings.
Note: Entire dish may be prepared just before serving, allowing about 1 hour.

WILD-RICE-AND-TURKEY CASSEROLE

1½ cups uncooked wild rice
4 cups boiling water
1 teaspoon salt
1 pound bulk pork sausage
1 3- or 4-ounce can whole
  mushrooms, undrained
2 10½-ounce cans con-
  densed cream-of-mush-
  room soup, undiluted

1 teaspoon Worcestershire
12 slices roast turkey or
  chicken
1½ cups day-old bread
  crumbs
¼ cup melted butter or
  margarine

Early on day:
1.   Wash rice; simmer in boiling water with salt, covered, 30 to 40 minutes, or until tender and water is absorbed; drain.
2.   Meanwhile, in skillet, cook sausage, over medium heat, until browned, stirring and breaking it into bits, and pouring off fat as it accumulates. Stir in mushrooms, soup, and Worcestershire; lightly stir this mixture into wild rice.
3.   Into well-greased 12-by-8-by-2-inch baking dish, spoon half of rice mixture; arrange turkey slices on top; then spoon on rest of rice mixture. Refrigerate.
About 40 minutes before serving:
1.   Start heating oven to 375°F.
2.   Mix crumbs with melted butter; sprinkle over rice in 1-inch border around edge of casserole.
3.   Bake about 30 minutes, or until hot and golden. Makes 8 servings.
FOR 4: Make ½ recipe; bake in 10-by-6-by-2-inch baking dish.

ITALIAN BAKED RICE

¼ cup butter or margarine
1 medium onion, minced
½ pound sweet Italian or
  ¾ pound fresh sausages,
  coarsely snipped
1 15-ounce can hearts of
  artichokes, drained,
  sliced
½ 10-ounce package
  frozen peas

1 3-ounce can broiled
  chopped mushrooms,
  drained
1 10½-ounce can con-
  densed beef bouillon,
  undiluted
3 cups cooked packaged
  precooked white rice
½ cup shredded Parmesan
  cheese

1.   Start heating oven to 375°F.
2.   In hot butter in large skillet, sauté onion and sausages until lightly browned. Add artichoke slices and peas; brown lightly.
3.   Add mushroom pieces and ½ cup beef bouillon. Simmer, uncovered, 10 minutes.
4.   Stir in rice and rest of bouillon; toss lightly. Turn into greased 1½-quart casserole. Sprinkle top with cheese.
5.   Bake 15 to 20 minutes, or until cheese is browned. Makes 4 servings.

SAVORY RICE AND CHEESE

¾ cup uncooked regular
  or processed white rice
2¼ teaspoons salt
2 tablespoons shortening
  or salad oil
½ cup diced celery
¼ cup minced green pepper

2 tablespoons minced onion
¼ teaspoon pepper
½ pound process sharp-
  Cheddar cheese, grated
  (2 cups)
⅔ cup milk

1.   In tightly covered saucepan combine rice, 1 teaspoon salt, and 2¼ cups boiling water. Cook, over low heat, 20 to 25 minutes, or until rice feels tender between fingers and all water is absorbed.
2.   Start heating oven to 425°F.
3.   In hot fat, in skillet, sauté celery, green pepper, and onion until tender-crisp; stir in 1¼ teaspoons salt and pepper.
4.   In greased 1½-quart casserole, arrange layers of rice, sautéed vegetables, and cheese, ending with cheese. Pour on milk.
5.   Bake, uncovered, 35 minutes, or until golden. Makes 4 servings.
FOR 2: Halve all ingredients; use 1-quart casserole.

BROWNED RICE AND PORK CASSEROLE

4 loin pork chops, ¾ inch
  thick
Seasoned salt
½ cup uncooked regular or
  processed white rice
1 10¾-ounce can beef
  gravy (1¼ cups)

¼ cup water
1 teaspoon salt
Dash pepper
4 medium onions
2 large carrots, cut
  diagonally into 1-inch
  slices

About 1 hour and 30 minutes before serving:
1.   Start heating oven to 350°F.
2.   Trim bit of fat from chops and heat in skillet. Sprinkle chops well with seasoned salt; then brown well on both sides in hot fat in skillet; remove chops to 2-quart casserole.
3.   Add rice to drippings in skillet; cook, stirring, until lightly browned; stir in beef gravy, water, salt, and pepper.

4. Arrange onions and carrots on top of chops; pour on gravy mixture.
5. Bake, uncovered, 1 hour, or until chops and vegetables are tender. Makes 4 servings.

ELEVEN-LAYERED CASSEROLE

1 8-ounce package elbow macaroni
Butter or margarine
2 large tomatoes, sliced (optional)
2 cups grated process sharp-Cheddar cheese
2 teaspoons salt
¼ teaspoon pepper
¼ teaspoon orégano
2 onions, thinly sliced
1 13-ounce can evaporated milk, undiluted
3 tablespoons grated Parmesan cheese

About 1 hour before serving:
1. Cook macaroni as package label directs; drain.
2. Start heating oven to 350°F.
3. Line sides of buttered 2-quart casserole with tomato slices, if desired. Arrange half of macaroni in bottom of casserole; cover with 1 cup grated Cheddar cheese.
4. Combine salt, pepper, and orégano; sprinkle half of it over cheese.
5. Arrange half of onion slices on top; then pour in 1 cup evaporated milk. Add remaining macaroni, Cheddar cheese, salt mixture, onion slices, and evaporated milk. Sprinkle with Parmesan cheese.
6. Bake 30 minutes, or until sides bubble and top is slightly browned.
7. Serve with frozen or canned mixed vegetables, curly-endive salad, and warm spiced baked pears for dessert. Makes 6 servings.

PORK-VEGETABLE CASSEROLE

2 tablespoons butter or margarine
2 cups chopped onions
1 teaspoon paprika
1½ pounds lean pork, ground
2 cups coarsely-chopped celery
2 cups coarsely-chopped green peppers
1 1-pound 12-ounce can tomatoes (about 3½ cups)
2 teaspoons seasoned salt
¼ teaspoon seasoned pepper
½ teaspoon monosodium glutamate
2 beef-bouillon cubes
1 8-ounce package elbow macaroni
½ cup grated Parmesan cheese

About 1 hour and 30 minutes before serving:
1. In large skillet, in hot butter, sauté onions until soft. Add paprika and pork; when golden, mix in celery, green peppers, tomatoes, seasoned salt, pepper, monosodium glutamate, and bouillon cubes; simmer, covered, 30 minutes.
2. Start heating oven to 350°F.
3. Meanwhile, cook macaroni as package label directs; drain. Toss with pork mixture. Pour into greased 3-quart casserole. Sprinkle with cheese.
4. Bake, uncovered, 30 minutes.
5. Serve with crisp French rolls, lime-gelatin fruit salad, sugar-topped sponge cupcakes, and coffee. Makes 8 to 10 servings.

POLKA-DOT BAKED MACARONI

2 cups elbow macaroni (8 ounces)
¼ cup butter or margarine
¼ cup regular all-purpose flour
1 10½-ounce can condensed cream-of-chicken soup, undiluted
1 cup milk
6 ounces process sharp-Cheddar cheese, grated (1½ cups)
1 10-ounce package frozen peas and carrots, thawed just enough to separate
1 tablespoon butter or margarine
⅛ teaspoon salt
1 tablespoon water

Early on day:
1. Cook macaroni as package label directs; drain.
2. Meanwhile, in saucepan melt ¼ cup butter; stir in flour, then soup and milk; cook, stirring, until thickened and smooth.
3. Combine macaroni, soup mixture, ¾ cup cheese, and half of peas and carrots. Turn into 3-quart greased casserole; sprinkle rest of cheese on top.
4. Place rest of peas and carrots in small casserole with 1 tablespoon butter, salt, and water. Refrigerate both casseroles.
About 40 minutes before serving:
1. Start heating oven to 400°F.
2. Bake macaroni, uncovered, and vegetables, covered, 30 minutes, or until bubbling hot and golden.
3. When done, spoon carrots and peas from small casserole around edge of macaroni. Makes 6 servings.

SUPPER IN A DISH

2 cups elbow macaroni
1 12-ounce can luncheon meat
Butter or margarine
3 tablespoons regular all-purpose flour
2½ cups milk
1½ teaspoons salt
¼ teaspoon pepper
1½ teaspoons prepared horse-radish
1 teaspoon prepared mustard
½ teaspoon Worcestershire
1 cup cooked or canned peas
2 tablespoons snipped parsley
½ cup shredded sharp-Cheddar cheese

About 1 hour and 30 minutes before serving:
1. Cook macaroni as package label directs; drain.
2. Start heating oven to 375°F.
3. Meanwhile, cut luncheon meat into thin strips, 1-

inch wide. In double boiler melt 3 tablespoons butter; stir in flour, then gradually stir in milk, salt, pepper, horse-radish, mustard, and Worcestershire. Cook, stirring, until thickened and smooth.

4. Stir sauce into macaroni; add luncheon meat, peas, and parsley; pour into greased 2-quart casserole. Sprinkle with cheese; dot with 1 tablespoon butter.

5. Bake 30 minutes, or until hot.

6. Serve with vegetable-juice cocktail, orange salad, brownies à la mode, and coffee. Makes 6 servings.

HAMBURGER UPSIDE-DOWN CASSEROLE
(Pictured here)

2½ cups elbow macaroni (about ¾ pound)	¼ teaspoon pepper
3 tablespoons butter or margarine	¼ teaspoon orégano
½ cup minced onion	1 8-ounce package process Cheddar cheese, grated
2 teaspoons minced garlic	3 eggs, beaten
1 pound chuck, ground	¾ cup milk
1 8-ounce can tomato sauce	1 or 2 10-ounce packages frozen asparagus spears
1 teaspoon salt	

Day before:

1. Cook macaroni as package label directs, until *just* tender; drain.

2. Meanwhile, in hot butter in large skillet, sauté onion and garlic until tender. Add chuck; cook, stirring constantly, until brown. Stir in tomato sauce, salt, pepper, and orégano; simmer a few minutes, then spread over bottom of greased 2-quart casserole.

3. Toss macaroni with grated cheese; arrange on top of meat-tomato mixture in casserole, packing it down.

4. Combine eggs and milk; pour over macaroni. Cover casserole with saran; refrigerate.

About 2 hours before serving:

1. Start heating oven to 350°F.

2. Let casserole stand out 15 minutes. Then bake 1 hour and 30 minutes, or until macaroni is golden and custard is set.

3. When done, remove casserole from oven and let stand 15 minutes. Then loosen around edges with spatula and carefully unmold onto serving platter.

4. Meanwhile, cook asparagus as package label directs; drain. Arrange some around unmolded casserole, with a few tips on top as pictured. Serve in pie-shaped wedges. Makes 6 servings.

SPAGHETTI-CHEESE CASSEROLE

¼ pound spaghetti, in pieces	1 1-pound can tomatoes
3 tablespoons butter or margarine	1 teaspoon salt
	¼ teaspoon pepper
2 tablespoons chopped celery	¼ teaspoon granulated sugar
2 tablespoons chopped green pepper	½ cup grated or shredded natural sharp-Cheddar cheese
2 tablespoons minced onion	4 frankfurters, sliced diagonally
3 tablespoons regular all-purpose flour	Green pepper rings (optional)

About 1 hour before serving:

1. Cook spaghetti as package label directs; drain. (There should be 2 cups cooked spaghetti.)

2. Start heating oven to 350°F.

Hamburger Upside-Down Casserole

3. In hot butter in large saucepan, over low heat, lightly brown celery, green pepper, and onion. Stir in flour. Add tomatoes, salt, pepper, sugar, and cheese, stirring just until cheese is melted. Remove from heat.
4. Stir in spaghetti and frankfurters; turn mixture into greased 1½-quart casserole.
5. Bake 30 minutes, or until bubbly and golden.
6. Garnish top of casserole with green pepper rings, if desired. Makes 2 or 3 servings.

FRENCH RAGOUT WITH OLIVES

1 cup spaghetti, in pieces	1 3- or 4-ounce can sliced
1 pound chuck, ground	mushrooms, drained
1 16- or 17-ounce can	1 cup ground pecans
tomatoes	3 tablespoons butter or
2 onions, chopped	margarine
2 green peppers, chopped	¼ cup grated Parmesan
7 stalks celery, chopped	cheese
1 teaspoon salt	1 4-ounce can pitted ripe
1 teaspoon pepper	olives
1 16- or 17-ounce can	
small peas	

About 1 hour and 30 minutes before serving:
1. Start heating oven to 350°F.
2. In Dutch oven, cook spaghetti as package label directs; drain.
3. Add chuck, tomatoes, onions, green peppers, celery, salt, pepper, peas with their liquid, mushrooms, and pecans. Mix well. Turn mixture into 3-quart casserole; dot top with butter. Sprinkle with cheese.
4. Bake, uncovered, about 1 hour, or until slightly browned and hot in center.
5. Garnish with drained olives. Serve with tossed all-green salad, French bread, snow pudding with custard sauce and grated chocolate, spice cookies, and coffee. Makes 6 servings.

CRAB MEAT, TETRAZZINI STYLE

1 8-ounce package	1 1-pound 2-ounce can
spaghetti	tomato juice
3 tablespoons butter or	2 6½-ounce cans crab
margarine	meat, flaked, or 2 6-
1 medium onion, minced	ounce packages frozen
⅓ cup chopped green	King crab meat, thawed,
pepper	well drained
1 pound fresh mushrooms,	2 8-ounce packages
sliced	shredded process
1 10¾-ounce can con-	Cheddar cheese
densed tomato soup,	
undiluted	

About 1 hour before serving:
1. Cook spaghetti as package label directs; drain.
2. Start heating oven to 350°F.

3. Meanwhile, in large skillet, melt butter; in it sauté onion, green pepper, and mushrooms until golden. Stir in soup, tomato juice, crab meat, and 1 package cheese; bring to boil.
4. In 13-by-9-by-2-inch baking dish arrange spaghetti; pour on crab-meat mixture; toss well. Sprinkle on other package of cheese.
5. Bake 40 minutes, or until golden and bubbly.
6. Serve with hot rolls, lettuce wedges with Russian dressing, and cherries flambé. Makes 8 servings.

SAVORY BAKED SPAGHETTI

3 tablespoons bacon fat or	1 1-pound 13-ounce can
salad oil	tomatoes (3½ cups)
2 medium onions, coarsely	1 teaspoon chili powder
chopped	1 cup water
1 clove garlic (optional)	1 8-ounce package
½ pound chuck, ground	spaghetti
1½ teaspoons salt	¼ pound process Cheddar
⅛ teaspoon pepper	cheese, grated (1 cup)

1. In fat in large skillet, cook onions and garlic 5 minutes. Add chuck; cook, stirring occasionally, until meat loses its red color. Stir in salt, pepper, and tomatoes. Simmer, covered, 30 minutes; discard garlic. Add chili powder and water.
2. Start heating oven to 325°F.
3. Break half of spaghetti into greased 2-quart casserole; pour on half of sauce; sprinkle with half of cheese. Repeat.
4. Bake, covered, 35 minutes; uncover, and bake 15 minutes longer, or until brown. Makes 6 servings.
FOR 2: Halve all ingredients; use 1-quart casserole.

CASSEROLE FROM THE SEA

About 2 cups packaged ziti	1 5-ounce can water
1 10½-ounce can con-	chestnuts, drained,
densed cream-of-mush-	sliced
room soup, undiluted	1 cup minced celery
⅓ cup mayonnaise	3 tablespoons snipped
⅓ cup milk	parsley
1 5-ounce can cleaned	1 teaspoon minced onion
shrimp	Curry powder
1 6½- or 7-ounce can tuna	

About 1 hour before serving:
1. Cook ziti as package label directs; drain.
2. Start heating oven to 350°F.
3. Meanwhile, in 2-quart casserole, combine soup, mayonnaise, and milk. Add shrimp, rinsed under cold water, tuna, water chestnuts, celery, parsley, onion, and ziti. Sprinkle lightly with curry powder.
4. Bake 30 minutes, or until hot.
5. Serve with spinach salad, French bread, ice cream with pineapple chunks, and cookies. Makes 4 servings.

Vegetable Casseroles

VEGETABLES EN CASSEROLE

½ cup water
1 10-ounce package frozen
   mixed vegetables
½ cup chopped onion
½ cup chopped celery
½ teaspoon seasoned salt
1 10½-ounce can
   condensed cream-of-
   mushroom soup,
   undiluted

½ cup packaged poultry-
   stuffing mix
½ teaspoon basil
½ teaspoon marjoram
2 tablespoons butter or
   margarine

About 45 minutes before serving:
1. In saucepan place water, mixed vegetables, onion, celery, and seasoned salt. Cook, uncovered, until vegetables are tender-crisp; drain thoroughly.
2. Start heating oven to 350°F.
3. Mix vegetables with soup; turn into 1-quart casserole. Combine stuffing mix, basil, marjoram, and butter; sprinkle over vegetable mixture.
4. Bake 30 minutes. Makes 4 servings.

RUFFLED ARTICHOKES ITALIAN
(Pictured on page 50)

4 artichokes
2 tablespoons lemon juice
1 clove garlic
Salt
2 tablespoons salad oil
1½ cups fresh bread
   crumbs

¾ cup grated Parmesan
   cheese
¼ teaspoon pepper
1 small onion, minced
¼ cup snipped parsley

About 1 hour and 15 minutes before serving:
1. Wash artichokes; trim stems to ½ inch. Pull off tough outer leaves; then, with kitchen scissors, snip one-third from top of each remaining leaf. Place artichokes, upside down, on surface, then firmly press end of each to open up leaves.
2. In deep saucepan, in 1 inch boiling water to which lemon and garlic have been added, stand artichokes, stem down, fitting them together snuggly so they hold shape. Over top of each sprinkle ¼ teaspoon salt, then a drizzle of salad oil. Cook, covered, 20 to 45 minutes, or until stems can be easily pierced with fork. Then lift out of water, and turn upside down to drain. Reserve ¼ cup water.
3. Meanwhile, make this stuffing: Mix crumbs, cheese, ½ teaspoon salt, pepper, onion, and parsley.

4. Start heating oven to 325°F.
5. To stuffing mixture add reserved cooking water; toss. Stand artichokes in 3-quart casserole; tuck bits of stuffing between artichoke leaves (don't worry if all are not filled).
6. Bake 20 minutes, or until stuffing is heated.
7. Lift out carefully; serve hot. Nice with steak. Makes 4 servings.

CHICKEN-STUFFED ARTICHOKES: Prepare artichokes as in steps 1 and 2, above. Then remove center leaves and scrape out choke with tip of teaspoon. Make twice recipe for stuffing in step 3. Use half to stuff artichokes as in step 5; to rest add 1 to 1½ cups cut-up cooked chicken; spoon into centers. Bake as directed above.

BEANS TRES BIEN

2 9-ounce packages frozen
   French-style green beans
1 3½-ounce can French-
   fried onions

1 10½-ounce can
   condensed cream-of-
   mushroom soup,
   undiluted

1. Start heating oven to 400°F.
2. Cook green beans 1 minute less than package label directs. Drain from them all but ½ cup liquid. Turn beans into 1½-quart casserole. Stir in onions and soup.
3. Bake about 10 minutes, or until bubbly. Makes 4 servings.

FRENCH STUFFED CABBAGE

1 medium head green
   cabbage
1 tablespoon butter or
   margarine
¼ cup minced onion
¼ pound bulk pork sausage
1 cup chopped cooked lamb
   or beef
2 tablespoons fresh bread
   crumbs

1 cup cooked rice
½ teaspoon salt
Dash pepper
1 clove garlic, minced
1 egg, beaten
1 carrot, sliced
1 onion, thinly sliced
2 bacon slices
2 cups canned tomatoes

1. In kettle, in boiling salted water to cover, simmer whole cabbage 5 minutes. Plunge into cold water; drain well.
2. Meanwhile, start heating oven to 400°F.
3. Prepare this stuffing: In hot butter, in small skillet, sauté minced onion until tender. Toss with meats, crumbs, rice, salt, pepper, and garlic; mix in egg.
4. In 3-quart casserole arrange carrot and onion slices; on them place 2 lengths of string (to be used for tying cabbage), then drained cabbage, stem end down. With knife, cut out 3-inch round center of cabbage to about 2 inches from bottom. Press stuffing into cavity.
5. Top cabbage with bacon slices; with string, tie head firmly together, pulling leaves up over stuffing. Around it, pour tomatoes.

6. Bake, covered, 1 hour and 30 minutes.
7. Cut string. Serve in casserole, cut into wedges. Makes 6 main-dish servings.

BUFFET CHEESE-SCALLOPED CARROTS

12 medium carrots, sliced
¼ cup butter or margarine
1 small onion, minced
¼ cup regular all-purpose flour
1 teaspoon salt
¼ teaspoon dry mustard
2 cups milk
⅛ teaspoon pepper
¼ teaspoon celery salt
½ pound package process sharp-Cheddar cheese slices
3 cups buttered fresh bread crumbs

1. Start heating oven to 350°F.
2. Cook carrots in 1 inch boiling salted water about 10 minutes; drain.
3. Meanwhile, in butter in saucepan, gently cook onion 2 or 3 minutes. Stir in flour, salt, mustard, then milk; cook, stirring, until smooth. Add pepper and celery salt.
4. In 2-quart casserole arrange layer of carrots, then layer of cheese slices. Repeat until both are used, ending with carrots. Pour on sauce; top with buttered bread crumbs.
5. Bake, uncovered, 25 minutes, or until golden. Makes 8 servings.
To do ahead: Make early in day; refrigerate. Bake, uncovered, 35 to 45 minutes, or until hot.

VEGETABLE CASSEROLE DE LUXE

1½ cups boiling water
Salt
2½ cups sliced carrots
2½ cups diced potatoes
½ cup chopped onion
1 1-pound can whole Blue Lake green beans
3 tablespoons butter or margarine
3 tablespoons regular all-purpose flour
3 tablespoons pasteurized process cheese spread
Dash pepper (optional)

About 50 minutes before serving:
1. In medium saucepan, in boiling water with 1 teaspoon salt, cook carrots, potatoes, and onion until tender —about 10 minutes. Drain, reserving liquid. Arrange vegetables in greased 2-quart casserole.
2. Drain green beans, reserving liquid.
3. In saucepan, over low heat, melt butter; blend in flour; slowly stir in all reserved vegetable liquids. Cook, stirring, until thickened and clear. Add cheese; stir until cheese is melted and sauce is smooth. Season to taste with salt and pepper.
4. Start heating oven to 425°F.
5. Pour half of cheese sauce over vegetables in casserole. Top with green beans; cover with rest of cheese sauce.
6. Bake casserole 20 minutes. Makes 6 servings.

CUSTARD CORN PUDDING

2 cups chopped, cooked or canned, whole-kernel corn
2 eggs, slightly beaten
1 teaspoon granulated sugar
1½ tablespoons melted butter or margarine
2 cups scalded milk
1¾ teaspoons salt
¼ teaspoon pepper

1. Start heating oven to 325°F.
2. Combine corn, eggs, sugar, butter, milk, salt, and pepper; pour into greased 1½-quart casserole. Set in pan of warm water.
3. Bake, uncovered, 1 hour and 15 minutes, or until set. Makes 6 servings.
FOR 2: Halve ingredients; use 3 individual casseroles.
To vary: Before baking pudding mixture, add ½ cup minced cooked ham or grated cheese, or 2 tablespoons minced onion.

GOLDEN-TOPPED BAKED BEANS

2 1-pound cans baked beans in tomato sauce
1 tablespoon minced onion
Prepared mustard
1 teaspoon horse-radish
8 uncooked Canadian-style bacon slices, ¼ inch thick
4 ¼-inch thick halved orange slices
¼ cup brown sugar, packed
1 tablespoon butter or margarine
Whole cloves

1. Start heating oven to 400°F.
2. In deep fluted 9-inch pie plate or shallow casserole (5-cup capacity), combine beans, onion, 1 teaspoon mustard, and horse-radish.
3. Spread bit of mustard on each bacon slice; arrange with orange slices, pin-wheel fashion, on top of beans. Sprinkle all with brown sugar; dot with butter; stud meat with cloves.
4. Bake 25 minutes. Makes 4 servings.
PINEAPPLE-STYLE: Make as above, substituting 4 halved, well-drained canned pineapple slices for orange slices. Substitute 1 12-ounce can luncheon meat, cut into 6 slices, for Canadian-style bacon.

SAVORY LIMA-BEAN POT

4 cups large California
  dry limas, rinsed
4 teaspoons salt
5 tablespoons butter or
  margarine
2 medium onions, sliced
1 green pepper, diced

½ cup catchup
½ cup molasses
2 tablespoons vinegar
½ teaspoon Tabasco
2 teaspoons dry mustard
1 to 3 cups diced cooked
  ham

1. Place rinsed limas and salt in 2 quarts boiling water; simmer, covered, 2 hours, or until tender (add more boiling water if needed).
2. Start heating oven to 325°F.
3. In 2 tablespoons butter sauté onions and green pepper until tender. Mix catchup with molasses, vinegar, tabasco, and mustard. When limas are tender, drain, reserving 1 cup liquid. Add this liquid to catchup mixture.
4. In 3-quart casserole or large bean pot, arrange, in layers, limas, onion mixture, and ham; pour on catchup mixture. Dot with 3 tablespoons butter.
5. Bake casserole, uncovered, 1 hour and 30 minutes. Wonderful dish to serve for a buffet. Makes 10 to 12 servings.

BOSTON-STYLE BEAN POT: Substitute 4 cups dried pea beans, soaked overnight, for dry limas; simmer only 1 hour. Use 2¾ cups liquid drained from beans instead of 1 cup. (When arranging layers, place beans on top.) Bake 2 hours and 30 minutes, or until beans are tender.

EGGPLANT PARMESAN
(Pictured opposite)

1 medium eggplant
1 egg, unbeaten
2 tablespoons water
½ to ¾ cup packaged
  dried bread crumbs
Salad oil
1 8-ounce can tomato sauce
½ teaspoon orégano

½ teaspoon Italian
  seasoning
½ teaspoon savory
½ cup grated Parmesan
  cheese
1 8-ounce package skim-
  milk Mozzarella cheese,
  sliced

About 1 hour before serving:
1. Start heating oven to 375°F.
2. Cut eggplant into ½-inch crosswise slices. Beat egg with water. Dip eggplant slices into egg mixture, then into bread crumbs.
3. In ¼ cup salad oil, in large skillet, sauté a few eggplant slices until they are brown on outside and fork-tender. Repeat, using ¼ cup oil each time, until all of eggplant slices have been sautéed.
4. Over bottom of greased 2-quart casserole, layer half of eggplant slices, then half of tomato sauce, orégano, Italian seasoning, savory, Parmesan and Mozzarella cheeses. Repeat.

5. Bake 30 to 40 minutes.
6. Serve with chicory salad, Italian green beans, snow pudding with custard sauce, and café au lait. Makes 4 to 6 servings.

STUFFED-PEPPER CASSEROLE

4 large green peppers,
  halved lengthwise
1½ cups cooked rice
¼ cup undiluted evaporated
  milk or light cream
1 cup grated sharp-Cheddar
  cheese (¼ pound)
½ teaspoon monosodium
  glutamate
Salt
Pepper
2 medium tomatoes, peeled

4 teaspoons butter or
  margarine
2 eggs, unbeaten
¼ cup light cream or milk
2 tablespoons melted
  butter or margarine
1½ cups cooked or canned
  corn (cream style or
  whole kernel)
1 cup coarsely-crumbled
  crackers
Paprika

Early on day:
1. Cook green peppers in boiling salted water 5 minutes; drain.
2. For rice stuffing, mix cooked rice, evaporated milk, cheese, and monosodium glutamate with salt and pepper to taste.
3. Cut tomatoes into thick slices; sprinkle with salt and pepper; stand a slice inside one end or inside each end of 4 pepper halves. Then fill 4 pepper halves with rice stuffing; dot top of each with 1 teaspoon butter.
4. For corn stuffing, beat eggs with fork. Add light cream, melted butter, corn, cracker crumbs, ½ teaspoon salt, and speck pepper.
5. Heap corn stuffing into 4 remaining pepper halves. Refrigerate all.
About 50 minutes before serving:
1. Start heating oven to 375°F.
2. Arrange filled pepper halves in greased shallow baking dish.
3. Bake, uncovered, about 30 minutes, or until corn stuffing is firm when tested with tip of knife.
4. Sprinkle each corn-stuffed pepper with a little paprika. Then serve one pepper half of each kind on each plate. Makes 4 servings.

JOHN J. LIMAS

1 10-ounce package frozen
  Fordhook limas
½ cup crumbled Roquefort
  or Danish blue cheese

¼ cup undiluted canned
  condensed consommé
2 tablespoons fresh bread
  crumbs
Snipped parsley

1. Cook limas as package label directs; drain.
2. Start heating oven to 350°F.
3. In greased 1-quart casserole, arrange limas and

Eggplant Parmesan

New Potatoes, Country Style, Green Peas Bonne Femme, Ruffled Artichokes Italian

cheese in layers, ending with limas. Pour on consommé; top with bread crumbs.

4. Bake 20 minutes; sprinkle with parsley. Makes 2 or 3 servings.

GREEN PEAS BONNE FEMME
(Pictured here)

4 pounds fresh green peas
   (about 4 cups shelled)
2 large lettuce leaves
3 or 4 parsley sprigs
About 6 scallions
3 tablespoons butter or margarine
½ pound medium fresh mushrooms
   sliced

¾ cup undiluted canned
   condensed consommé
¼ cup sherry
1½ teaspoons salt
¼ teaspoon pepper
½ teaspoon nutmeg
¼ teaspoon marjoram
1 teaspoon granulated sugar

Early on day, or 2 hours before serving:
1. Shell peas, discarding any shoots; wash and drain.
2. Line ends of 1½-quart deep oval casserole with lettuce leaves. Tie parsley sprigs together.
3. Snip scallions into 1½-inch pieces. In butter, in medium skillet, over medium heat, sauté mushrooms with scallions until golden. Remove from heat; add peas, then toss; spoon into casserole.
4. Heat consommé with sherry; stir in salt, pepper, nutmeg, marjoram, and sugar. Pour over peas; top with parsley; refrigerate.
About 1 hour and 15 minutes before serving:
1. Start heating oven to 375°F.
2. Remove casserole from refrigerator; stir up contents.
3. Bake, covered, 50 to 60 minutes, or until peas are tender-crisp.
4. Uncover; discard lettuce and parsley; stir and serve. Makes 5 to 7 servings.

STUFFED ONION ROLLS

2 large yellow onions, peeled
Salt
2 tablespoons butter or margarine
¾ pound veal shoulder, ground
1 tablespoons regular all-purpose
   flour

1 egg, unbeaten
¼ teaspoon white pepper
1 cup heavy cream
Parsley sprigs

About 1 hour before serving:
1. Boil onions in plenty of salted boiling water about 10 minutes.
2. Start heating oven to 425°F.
3. Melt butter; pour it into 1½-quart shallow casserole. With paring knife, make a slit from top to bottom of each onion through just to center. Peel off each layer of onion; dip outer side in butter, then arrange in rows, in casserole, outer-side down and hollow-side up, each one forming a cup for filling.
4. Combine veal, flour, egg, 1½ teaspoons salt, and pepper. Stir in cream, ¼ cup at a time, mixing thoroughly. Place about 2 tablespoons of this stuffing mixture in each onion leaf. Fold onion leaves around stuffing to make small oval-shaped rolls; place in casserole so edges are down.
5. Bake 20 to 30 minutes, basting with drippings.
6. Serve, garnished with parsley, with cucumber-tomato salad, corn on the cob, hot biscuits, orange ice, and coffee. Makes 4 servings.

ALMOND-ONION CASSEROLE

2 15½-ounce cans whole
 onions, drained
1½ tablespoons butter or
 margarine
1½ tablespoons regular
 all-purpose flour
½ cup canned cream-of-
 mushroom soup,
 undiluted

½ cup shredded sharp-
 Cheddar cheese
½ cup toasted slivered
 almonds
¼ teaspoon monosodium
 glutamate
¼ cup sherry

1. Start heating oven to 350°F.
2. Place onions in buttered 1-quart casserole.
3. In small saucepan melt butter; stir in flour, soup, cheese, ¼ cup almonds, monosodium glutamate, and sherry. Pour mixture over onions; sprinkle with remaining almonds.
4. Bake, uncovered, 30 minutes. Makes 4 servings.
To do ahead: Day before, make casserole—all but final sprinkling with almonds; refrigerate. Add nuts just before baking; bake 45 minutes.

NEW POTATOES, COUNTRY STYLE
(Pictured on page 50)

2½ to 3 pounds small new
 potatoes, unpeeled
½ cup butter or margarine
3 tablespoons regular all-
 purpose flour
1 teaspoon salt
¼ teaspoon pepper

2 cups water
½ pound bacon slices
1 tablespoon lemon juice
Snipped fresh dill or
 chives
Snipped parsley

About 45 minutes before serving:
1. Cook potatoes, covered, in boiling salted water 20 minutes, or until tender.
2. Meanwhile, make butter sauce: In saucepan, over low heat, melt butter; stir in flour, salt, and pepper; slowly stir in water. Cook, stirring, until thickened.
3. Start heating oven to 325°F.
4. In large skillet, over low heat, fry bacon until crisp but not brittle, turning with 2 forks and spooning off fat as it accumulates. Drain bacon on paper towels.
5. When potatoes are tender, drain, and, if desired,

remove small band of skin around center of each as pictured on page 50. Heap in skillet with ovenproof handle or 1½-quart shallow casserole.
6. Into butter sauce, stir lemon juice; pour over potatoes.
7. Bake 20 minutes.
8. Top with 6 slices crisp bacon; sprinkle generously with dill and parsley. Pass rest of bacon. Makes 6 servings.

POTATO TART

3 medium potatoes, pared,
 cut up
Salt
¼ teaspoon pepper
¼ cup salad oil
3 medium tomatoes, sliced

½ pound Mozzarella
 cheese slices
½ teaspoon rosemary
3 tablespoons grated
 Parmesan cheese

About 1 hour before serving:
1. Start heating oven to 400°F.
2. Cook potatoes, in boiling water to cover, until tender. Drain, mash, then combine with 1 teaspoon salt and pepper. Spread over bottom of 8-by-8-by-2-inch baking dish.
3. Pour on half of salad oil. Top with alternate rows of tomato and Mozzarella slices. Sprinkle with ¾ teaspoon salt, rosemary, and Parmesan cheese. Pour on rest of oil.
4. Bake 35 to 40 minutes, or until golden.
5. Serve with broiled lamb steaks, spiced cling-peach halves on water cress, nuts, and demitasse. Makes 6 servings.

GNOCCHI AU GRATIN

4 cups cold mashed
 potatoes (2 to 2½
 pounds potatoes)
1½ cups unsifted regular
 all-purpose flour
6 egg yolks, unbeaten
Salt
¼ teaspoon pepper

1 teaspoon prepared
 mustard
5 2½-ounce jars shredded
 Parmesan cheese
6 quarts hot water
½ cups melted butter or
 margarine

1. Start heating oven to 350°F.
2. In large bowl combine potatoes, flour, egg yolks, 2 teaspoons salt, pepper, mustard, and 4 jars cheese.
3. In large kettle, bring hot water to slow boil; add 1 tablespoon salt.
4. Place some of potato mixture in large pastry bag, with plain tube number 8 in place. Holding bag over simmering water, force contents through tube, snipping off ¾-inch pieces. Cook gently until they rise to surface (they are done). Remove at once; drain on paper towels. Place in buttered 1½-quart casserole; keep warm in oven. Repeat until all potato mixture is used.

5. Remove casserole from oven; turn on broiler. Pour butter over gnocchi, then sprinkle with remaining jar of cheese. Broil until golden—about 5 minutes. Makes 12 servings.

SWISS FAMILY CASSEROLE

Butter or margarine	2½ teaspoons salt
½ cup snipped parsley	½ teaspoon pepper
2 cups chopped onion	3 tablespoons regular all-
2½ pounds potatoes, pared, cooked, then cut in ¼-inch slices	purpose flour
	2 cups commercial sour cream
4 hard-cooked eggs, sliced	1½ cups grated Cheddar cheese
4 medium, ripe tomatoes, in ¼-inch slices	⅛ teaspoon paprika
	1 cup fresh bread crumbs

About 1 hour before serving:

1. Start heating oven to 350°F.
2. In ¼ cup melted butter, in skillet, sauté parsley and onion until tender.
3. In 3-quart casserole arrange half of potatoes; cover with egg slices, then onion mixture. Arrange tomato slices in layer; sprinkle with 1½ teaspoons salt and ¼ teaspoon pepper; then top with rest of potatoes.
4. Into 2 tablespoons melted butter, in same skillet, stir flour, then sour cream and 1 cup cheese. Add 1 teaspoon salt, ¼ teaspoon pepper, and paprika. Cook until mixture is thickened; pour over potatoes. Sprinkle with crumbs and remaining cheese; dot with 2 tablespoons butter.
5. Bake 30 minutes. Makes 6 generous servings.

FOR 4: Make as above, halving all ingredients; use 1½-quart casserole.

MERLE'S COMPANY CASSEROLE

1 cup fresh bread crumbs	3 tablespoons butter or margarine
1 pimento, coarsely chopped	3 tablespoons regular all-
2 tablespoons snipped parsley	purpose flour
	1½ teaspoons salt
3 small zucchini, thinly sliced	¼ teaspoon pepper
1 large onion, sliced	2 cups milk
1 12-ounce can whole-kernel corn, drained	1 egg yolk, well beaten

1. Start heating oven to 350°F.
2. Line bottom of 1½-quart casserole with half of crumbs. Combine pimento and parsley.
3. In casserole, alternate layers of zucchini, onion, and corn until all are used. Top with pimento-parsley mixture.
4. In saucepan, melt 2 tablespoons butter; stir in flour, salt, and pepper. Gradually add milk. Cook, stirring constantly, until mixture is thickened. Cool slightly.
5. Into sauce, stir egg yolk; pour over vegetables. Sprinkle with remaining crumbs; dot with 1 tablespoon butter.
6. Bake 35 minutes, or until fork-tender. Makes 6 servings.

SUMMER SQUASH EN CASSEROLE

2 pounds summer squash	2 tablespoons butter or margarine
1 teaspoon salt	
⅛ teaspoon pepper	

1. Start heating oven to 400°F.
2. Wash squash; cut into ½-inch slices. Place in layers in greased 2-quart casserole, sprinkling each layer with some of salt and pepper, and dotting with some of butter, until all is used.
3. Bake, covered, 1 hour, or until tender. Makes 4 servings.

SCALLOPED TOMATOES

3 tablespoons butter or margarine	1 teaspoon salt
	¼ teaspoon pepper
¼ cup minced onion	Dash cayenne pepper
2¼ cups fresh bread crumbs	1 1-pound 13-ounce can tomatoes (3½ cups)
½ teaspoon granulated sugar	1 tablespoon melted butter or margarine

1. Start heating oven to 375°F.
2. In 3 tablespoons butter, in small saucepan, sauté onion until tender. Add 2 cups bread crumbs, sugar, salt, pepper, and cayenne.
3. Arrange layer of tomatoes in greased 1½-quart casserole. Top with layer of onion-bread mixture; repeat until all is used, ending with tomatoes.
4. Combine ¼ cup crumbs with melted butter; sprinkle over tomatoes.
5. Bake, uncovered, 45 minutes. Makes 5 or 6 servings.

FOR 2: Halve all ingredients; use 1-quart casserole. Proceed as directed.

JAMAICAN YAM CASSEROLE

1 1-pound can yams, drained	⅛ teaspoon pepper
	2 tablespoons coarsely-chopped pecans
½ medium banana, thickly sliced	2 tablespoons toasted flaked coconut
¼ cup orange juice	
½ teaspoon salt	

1. Start heating oven to 350°F.
2. In buttered 1-quart casserole, arrange yams and banana. Pour juice over all. Sprinkle with salt and pepper. Top with pecans and coconut.
3. Bake, covered, 30 minutes. Makes 2 servings.

Casserole Breads

CASSEROLE BANANA BREAD

2 cups sifted regular all-purpose flour	2 eggs, unbeaten
1 teaspoon baking soda	1⅓ cups mashed bananas (about 3)
1½ teaspoons salt	¼ to ½ cup chopped walnuts
½ cup butter or margarine	
⅔ cup granulated sugar	

Make day before:
1. Start heating oven to 350°F.
2. Sift flour with baking soda and salt.
3. In large saucepan, over low heat, melt butter; remove from heat. Stir in sugar, eggs, bananas, then flour mixture, until just blended; stir in walnuts. Turn into greased 1½-quart oval casserole.
4. Bake 1 hour, or until cake tester, inserted in center, comes out clean.
5. Cool bread 10 minutes in casserole, then turn out on wire rack to finish cooling. Wrap tightly in foil until serving time next day. Makes 1 loaf.

FRUITED SODA BREAD
(Pictured opposite)

4 cups sifted regular all-purpose flour	2 cups seedless raisins
¼ cup granulated sugar	½ cup halved candied cherries
1 teaspoon salt	¼ cup diced preserved orange peel
1 teaspoon double-acting baking powder	1⅓ cups buttermilk
2 tablespoons caraway seeds	1 egg, unbeaten
¼ cup butter or margarine softened	1 teaspoon baking soda
	1 egg yolk, lightly beaten with few drops water

About 3 hours before serving:
1. Start heating oven to 375°F.
2. Into 3-quart bowl sift flour with sugar, salt and baking powder; stir in caraway seeds. With pastry blender, or 2 knives, cut in butter until like coarse corn meal; stir in raisins, cherries, and orange peel.
3. In pint measure or small bowl blend buttermilk well with unbeaten egg and baking soda. Stir into flour mixture until just moistened.
4. Turn dough onto floured surface; knead lightly until smooth. Shape into oval loaf to fit greased 1½-quart shallow oval baking dish. With kitchen scissors or small sharp knife, cut a cross in top of loaf, about ½ inch deep, and running almost to ends of loaf. With

pastry brush, brush top and sides of loaf with egg yolk mixed with water.
5. Bake bread 50 minutes. Then cover top of loaf with foil, and bake 10 to 20 minutes longer, or until cake tester, inserted in center, comes out clean.
6. Cool bread in baking dish 10 minutes, then turn out, on side, on wire rack to finish cooling. To keep bread fresh, store tightly wrapped in saran or foil. Delicious toasted. Makes 1 loaf.

BANANA BATTER BREAD
(Pictured opposite)

⅓ cup scalded milk	2 medium bananas, mashed
½ cup granulated sugar	2 eggs, unbeaten
1 teaspoon salt	4½ cups sifted regular all-purpose flour
6 tablespoons butter or margarine	½ cup finely-chopped peanuts
½ cup very warm water	
3 packages active dry, or cakes, yeast	

Early on day:
1. In large bowl, combine milk, sugar, salt, and butter; cool to lukewarm.
2. Onto very warm water, in small bowl, sprinkle yeast; stir until dissolved; add to cooled milk mixture.
3. Add bananas, eggs, and 2 cups flour; with mixer at medium speed, beat 2 minutes (or with spoon for 300 vigorous strokes). Stir in remaining flour and ¼ cup peanuts; beat vigorously with spoon until well mixed. Cover bowl; let rise in warm place, free from drafts, until doubled in bulk—about 45 minutes.
4. Start heating oven to 400°F.
5. With spoon, stir down batter; beat 25 strokes. Turn into well-greased oval 2-quart casserole. Sprinkle remaining peanuts on top.
6. Bake about 45 minutes, or until done.
7. Turn out, on side, on wire rack to cool. Makes 1 loaf.

CHEESE SOUFFLÉ BREAD
(Pictured opposite)

1 cup milk	½ pound natural sharp-Cheddar cheese
2 tablespoons granulated sugar	½ cup very warm water
2 teaspoons salt	3 packages active dry, or cakes, yeast
1 tablespoon shortening	1 cup lukewarm water
6¾ cups sifted regular all-purpose flour	

Early on day:
1. In large saucepan scald milk; stir in sugar, salt, and shortening; cool to lukewarm.
2. Stir in 2 cups flour; beat until smooth. Coarsely grate cheese over dough; stir in cheese.

Fruited Soda Bread, Banana Batter Bread,
Cheese Soufflé Bread, Casserole-Rye Batter Bread

3. Onto very warm water, in small bowl, sprinkle yeast; stir until dissolved, then stir into cheese mixture.

4. Stir in lukewarm water, mixing well. Add 4 cups flour, all at once; stir vigorously until smooth.

5. Sprinkle some of remaining flour onto flat surface; turn out dough and knead until smooth and elastic—about 20 minutes, sprinkling with remaining flour as needed to keep dough from sticking. Dough should be rounded and satiny smooth.

6. Place dough in well-greased large bowl, then turn in bowl to grease all sides. Cover; let rise in warm place, free from drafts, until doubled in bulk—about 45 minutes.

7. Start heating oven to 400°F.

8. Punch down dough, then knead, right in bowl, until smooth and satiny. Place, seam side down, in well-greased 2-quart soufflé dish or casserole.

9. Bake about 50 minutes, or until done.

10. Turn cheese bread out, on side, on wire rack to cool. Makes 1 loaf.

SPOON BREAD
(Pictured on page 30)

1 quart milk	2 tablespoons butter or
1 cup water-ground or	margarine
regular corn meal	4 eggs, unbeaten
1½ teaspoons salt	

1. In double boiler heat milk; stir in corn meal and salt; cook, stirring, until thick mush.

2. Meanwhile, start heating oven to 425°F.

3. Remove mush from heat; add butter.

4. In medium bowl, beat eggs until well blended; slowly stir into mush. Pour into well-greased 1½-quart casserole.

5. Bake, uncovered, 50 to 55 minutes.

6. Serve at once from casserole, as the bread of the meal, with lots of butter or margarine. Makes 4 or 5 servings.

CASSEROLE-RYE BATTER BREAD
(Pictured on page 55)

1 cup milk	2 packages active dry, or
3 tablespoons granulated	cakes, yeast
sugar	2 teaspoons caraway seeds
1 tablespoon salt	3 cups sifted regular all-
1½ tablespoons shortening	purpose flour
1 cup very warm water	1½ cups unsifted rye flour
	2 teaspoons milk

Early on day:

1. In small saucepan scald 1 cup milk; stir in sugar, salt, and shortening; cool to lukewarm. Turn into large bowl.

2. Onto very warm water, in small bowl, sprinkle

yeast; stir until dissolved, then stir into lukewarm milk mixture along with 1 teaspoon caraway seeds.

3. To milk mixture add all-purpose and rye flours, all at once; stir until well blended. Cover bowl; let rise in warm place, free from drafts, until doubled in bulk—about 50 minutes.

4. Start heating oven to 400°F.

5. Stir batter down, then beat vigorously about 30 seconds. Turn into well-greased 1½-quart casserole. Brush top with 2 teaspoons milk; sprinkle with 1 teaspoon caraway seeds.

6. Bake about 50 minutes, or until done.

7. Turn out, on side, on wire rack to cool. Makes 1 loaf.

Go-Alongs

Here is a far-out-of-the-ordinary accompaniment for hot or cold ham, lamb, poultry, etc. Serve it warm, sweet, and pungent.

CURRIED-FRUIT BAKE
(Pictured opposite)

2 1-pound 13-ounce cans	6 bottled maraschino
cling-peach halves	cherries with stems
1 1-pound 4-ounce can	½ cup butter or margarine
pineapple slices	1 cup light-brown sugar,
1 1-pound 13-ounce can	packed
pear halves	6 teaspoons curry powder

Make day before:

1. Start heating oven to 325°F.

2. Drain fruits; dry well on paper towels; arrange in 2-quart shallow baking dish.

3. Melt butter; add brown sugar and curry powder. Spoon over fruit.

4. Bake, uncovered, 1 hour. Refrigerate.

About 30 minutes before serving:

Reheat casserole at 350°F. 30 minutes, or until hot. Serve warm, as an accompaniment with meat. Makes 20 servings.

FOR 12: Use 1 16-ounce can peach halves, 1 1-pound 4-ounce can pineapple slices, 1 16-ounce can pear halves, 5 maraschino cherries, ⅓ cup butter, ¾ cup brown sugar, and 4 teaspoons curry powder. Bake in 1½-quart casserole as above.

CURRIED APRICOTS: In pie plate arrange 1 16-ounce can apricot halves, drained. Combine 2 tablespoons melted butter or margarine, ¼ cup light-brown sugar,

Curried-Fruit Bake

packed, and 1½ teaspoons curry powder. Spoon mixture over fruit. Bake at 350°F. 30 minutes. Serve warm. Makes 6 servings.

CURRIED PEARS: In pie plate arrange 1 16-ounce can or 1 1-pound 1-ounce jar pear slices, drained. Combine 1 tablespoon melted butter or margarine with 1 tablespoon light-brown sugar. Add ¼ teaspoon curry powder. Spoon mixture over pears. Bake at 325°F. 25 minutes.

Rice is an ideal go-along, especially when you're casseroling. Bake it at the same time.

CASSEROLE RICE

1 cup uncooked regular white rice	1½ cups boiling water
1 teaspoon salt	Butter or margarine

1. In 1½-quart casserole combine rice with salt and boiling water. (Use 2 cups water if it's raw processed white rice.)
2. Bake, covered, along with one of casseroles, during the last 30 minutes.
3. Fluff up with fork, adding butter if desired. Makes 3 cups (if regular); 4 cups (if processed).
Note: For *packaged precooked rice,* use 2 cups rice to 2 cups hot water and 1 teaspoon salt. Bake, covered, during last 15 minutes with casserole. Fluff up with 2 teaspoons butter. Makes 4 cups.

How proud you'll be as they stand, majestically high and lovely, in individual casseroles, or on dinner plates, with roast beef.

YORKSHIRE PUDDINGS

1¼ cups sifted regular all-purpose flour	2 tablespoons hot melted butter or hot fat
1 teaspoon salt	drippings from roast beef
1½ cups milk	
2 eggs, unbeaten	

About 10 minutes before roast comes out of oven:
1. Into bowl sift flour and salt; with mixer at medium speed, gradually beat in milk, then eggs, until smooth.
2. Pour 1 teaspoon *hot* melted butter into each of 6 1½-cup individual casseroles or 10½-ounce-deep pie dishes. Pour in popoverlike batter.
3. Meanwhile, remove roast beef; turn oven temperature up to 450°F.
4. Immediately bake puddings 20 to 25 minutes, or until puffy and tops are tinged with deep brown.
5. Serve, piping hot, right in individual casseroles, or remove puddings from casseroles to dinner plates. Makes 6 servings.

Casserole Desserts

BREAD-AND-BUTTER CUSTARD PUDDING

4 bread slices, buttered	Granulated sugar
Seedless raisins	2 eggs, unbeaten
Cinnamon	1½ cups milk

About 50 minutes before serving:
1. Start heating oven to 400°F.
2. Place 1 bread slice, buttered side down, in 1-quart casserole. Sprinkle with a few raisins, then with cinnamon and sugar. Repeat with two more layers; top with last bread slice, buttered side up.
3. Beat eggs with milk; pour over bread. Sprinkle top with more cinnamon and sugar.
4. Bake 40 minutes, or until puffy and golden. Makes 3 servings.

APPLE CHARLOTTE WITH VANILLA SAUCE

1 package regular vanilla pudding-and-pie-filling mix	¼ cup seedless dark raisins
3½ cups milk	⅓ cup apricot preserves
About 3 pounds apples	11 slices white bread
½ cup water	¾ cup melted butter or margarine
¾ cup granulated sugar	½ teaspoon cinnamon

About 3 hours before serving:
1. Cook pudding mix as package label directs, using 3½ cups milk. Pour into serving bowl; place wax paper directly on surface; refrigerate.
2. Wash, core, and pare apples; cut apples into thin slices.
3. In large saucepan cook apples with water, ¼ cup sugar, and raisins, covered, about 15 minutes, or until tender; stir in apricot preserves; set aside.
4. Start heating oven to 375°F.
5. Brush both sides of bread slices with melted butter. On wax paper combine ½ cup sugar with cinnamon; into this mixture dip buttered bread slices.
6. Place 1 bread slice in bottom of 2-quart casserole. Stand up 4 more slices around sides, trimming them if necessary, so they are even with top of casserole. Then, from 4 more slices, cut 4 triangular-shaped pieces that fit into empty spaces around sides of casserole.
7. Spoon half of apple mixture into casserole. Top with all of bread left from cutting triangular-shaped pieces. Top with rest of apple mixture, then with 2 bread slices, cut in half diagonally.

8. Bake 40 minutes, or until golden brown and caramelized.

9. Serve warm, in wedges, topped with pudding sauce. Makes 6 to 8 servings.

Note: If desired, charlotte can be made early in day and served at room temperature.

BANANA-COCONUT BETTY

2 cups fresh bread crumbs
⅓ cup melted butter or
   margarine
4 medium bananas, thinly
   sliced
⅓ cup granulated sugar
½ teaspoon nutmeg

½ teaspoon cinnamon
1 tablespoon grated lemon
   peel
3 tablespoons lemon juice
¼ cup water
½ cup flaked coconut
Pour cream

About 1 hour before serving:

1. Start heating oven to 375°F.

2. Toss bread crumbs with melted butter. In greased 1½-quart casserole arrange one third of crumb mixture; cover with half of sliced bananas, then half of combined sugar, nutmeg, cinnamon, and lemon peel.

3. Top with another third of crumbs, rest of bananas, and rest of sugar mixture. Spoon on combined lemon juice and water. Combine rest of crumbs and coconut; top casserole with coconut-crumb mixture.

4. Bake, covered, 30 minutes; uncover; bake 2 to 5 minutes longer, or until golden.

5. Serve warm, with pour cream or whipped cream, sprinkled with cinnamon. Makes 6 servings.

PEACH-RICE CASSEROLE

1 1-pound 13-ounce can
   cling-peach slices
¼ cup granulated sugar
½ teaspoon salt
2½ cups milk
2 eggs, unbeaten

¾ teaspoon mace
½ teaspoon almond extract
2 cups cooked rice
2 tablespoons brown sugar
Pour cream (optional)

About 1 hour and 30 minutes before serving:

1. Drain peach slices thoroughly.

2. Start heating oven to 350°F.

3. In double boiler, over hot, *not boiling,* water, combine sugar with salt, milk, eggs, and mace. Cook, stirring constantly with wire whip or metal spoon, about 20 minutes, or until slightly thickened. Remove from heat; stir in almond extract, then rice.

4. Into buttered 2-quart casserole pour half of rice mixture; top with half of peach slices; repeat layers. Sprinkle top with brown sugar.

5. Bake, covered, 30 minutes, or until rice custard is hot and set.

6. Cool casserole, covered. Serve warm or cold, with pour cream. Makes 6 servings.

GINGER-BAKED PEARS AND APRICOTS

1 1-pound 14-ounce can
   pear halves
1 1-pound 14-ounce can
   whole apricots

2 tablespoons slivered
   crystallized ginger
4 lemon slices, halved

About 1 hour or more before serving:

1. Start heating oven to 325°F.

2. Drain pears, reserving ¾ cup syrup; arrange pears in 2-quart round casserole. Drain apricots; arrange in center of nest of pears.

3. Sprinkle slivered crystallized ginger over pears and apricots; tuck in lemon slices; pour syrup from pears over all.

4. Bake, uncovered, 30 minutes.

5. Serve cold. Makes 6 servings.

CHOCOLATEY-CREAM BREAD PUDDING
(Pictured on page 60)

7½ cups milk
6 squares unsweetened
   chocolate
1 teaspoon salt
6 eggs, unbeaten
1½ cups granulated sugar
2 tablespoons vanilla
   extract

½ teaspoon almond extract
10 slices stale bread,
   cut into ¼-inch cubes
¼ cup granulated sugar
Shaved unsweetened
   chocolate

Early on day:

1. Start heating oven to 400°F.

2. Place milk in saucepan; add squares chocolate and salt. Heat, over low heat, until chocolate is melted. With hand beater, beat until blended.

3. In large bowl, place 4 whole eggs and 2 egg yolks (put 2 egg whites in small bowl; set aside). Slightly beat eggs with yolks, then stir in 1½ cups sugar. Gradually fold in chocolate mixture thoroughly. Add vanilla and almond extracts, then bread cubes; let stand about 10 minutes.

4. Now turn chocolate mixture into 3-quart casserole; set it in pan of hot water that comes up halfway on side of casserole.

Chocolatey-Cream Bread Pudding

Chocolate-Vanilla Soufflé

5. Bake 1 hour.

6. Beat egg whites until foamy. Add ¼ cup sugar, 2 tablespoons at a time, beating after each addition until sugar is well blended in. Continue beating until stiff peaks form when beater is raised.

7. Lightly pile meringue in mounds, as border around top edge of pudding as pictured. Return pudding to oven for 5 to 10 minutes, or until meringue is delicately browned.

8. Remove pudding from oven; sprinkle meringue lightly with shaved chocolate. Serve warm or cool, with pour cream, if desired. Makes 8 to 10 servings.

FOR 4 OR 5: Make pudding as directed above, using 3¾ cups milk, 3 squares unsweetened chocolate, ½ teaspoon salt, 2 eggs, 2 egg yolks, ¾ cup granulated sugar, 1 teaspoon vanilla extract, ¼ teaspoon almond extract, and 5 slices stale bread, cubed. Bake in 1½-quart casserole 1 hour. Then top with meringue made from 2 egg whites and ¼ cup granulated sugar, and bake 5 to 10 minutes longer.

CHOCOLATE-MILK BREAD PUDDING

2 cups chocolate-milk dairy drink	½ teaspoon vanilla extract
1 cup day-old bread cubes	½ teaspoon almond extract
2 eggs, unbeaten	1 cup flaked coconut
¼ cup granulated sugar	Vanilla or coffee ice cream;
¼ teaspoon salt	or whipped cream or dessert topping

Day before (if served cold), or 1 hour before serving (if served hot):
1. Start heating oven to 350°F.
2. Scald chocolate-milk drink; add bread cubes.
3. In greased 1-quart casserole, beat eggs slightly. Add sugar, salt, vanilla and almond extracts. Stir in bread mixture, then coconut. Set casserole in shallow pan of hot water.
4. Bake 50 minutes, or until silver knife, inserted in center, comes out clean.
5. Serve pudding hot, topped with ice cream; or refrigerate and serve next day, cold, with whipped cream or dessert topping. Makes 4 to 6 servings.

CREAMY BAKED RICE PUDDING

1 quart milk	¼ teaspoon salt
¼ cup granulated sugar	¼ teaspoon nutmeg
¼ cup uncooked regular white rice	1 teaspoon vanilla extract
1 tablespoon butter or margarine	½ cup light or dark raisins (optional)

1. Start heating oven to 325°F.
2. In greased 1½-quart casserole combine milk, sugar, rice, butter, salt, nutmeg, and vanilla.
3. Bake, uncovered, stirring often, 2 hours and 30 minutes, or until rice is done. Add raisins after first hour of baking time.

4. Serve warm or cold, with pour cream, whipped cream, custard sauce flavored with rum, fudge sauce, caramel sauce, berries, fruit, or maple sugar. Makes 4 to 6 servings.

CHOCOLATE-VANILLA SOUFFLÉ
(Pictured opposite)

5 eggs	2 teaspoons vanilla extract
About 1 tablespoon soft butter or margarine	¼ teaspoon salt
	1 cup milk
5 squares semisweet chocolate	2 tablespoons cornstarch
⅓ cup heavy cream	Soft vanilla ice cream (optional)
½ cup granulated sugar	

About 2 hours before serving:
1. Set eggs and butter out to come to room temperature.
2. Place 1 inch of water in small roasting pan; set in oven. Start heating oven to 350°F.
3. Fold 30-inch length of foil, 12 inches wide, in half lengthwise; wrap around outside of round casserole, which measures 6 cups to brim, so collar 3 inches high stands above rim; fasten with cellophane tape. Generously butter inside surface of foil collar only.
4. In double-boiler top, over very hot, *not boiling*, water, melt chocolate; remove from heat. Stir in heavy cream.
5. Separate eggs, placing 4 yolks in small bowl, 5 whites in large one. (Reserve extra egg yolk for later use.) To yolks add ¼ cup sugar, vanilla, and salt. With mixer at high speed, beat until light-colored—about 3 minutes.
6. In small saucepan, with wire whip or metal spoon, blend milk and cornstarch. Boil, over high heat, stirring briskly, 1 minute. Remove from heat; beat into egg yolks, beating until smooth.
7. Pour chocolate into casserole; with rubber spatula, spread partially up sides of dish in 7 or 8 scallops; keep rest of dish free of chocolate.
8. With mixer at high speed, beat egg whites until foamy. Gradually add ¼ cup sugar, beating until soft peaks form.
9. With rubber spatula, fold egg-yolk mixture, all at once, into egg whites. Gently pour this mixture over chocolate layer, filling casserole. Set casserole in pan of hot water in oven.
10. Bake, *without peeking*, 60 to 65 minutes, or until set and browned. (Soufflé may or may not split on top.)
11. Spoon ice cream into bowl; refrigerate.
12. When soufflé is done, remove from oven; quickly, but gently, remove foil collar. Serve at once, spooning to bottom of soufflé for sauce; pass ice cream. Makes 6 servings.

Low-Calorie Casseroles

HAM AND POTATO CASSEROLE

1 tablespoon butter or
  margarine
1 12-ounce can spiced
  luncheon meat, cut in
  ½-inch cubes
1 small onion, minced
2 tablespoons chopped
  green pepper
1 cup sliced celery

¼ cup regular all-purpose
  flour
2 cups skim milk or
  reliquefied nonfat
  dry milk
5 cups pared, diced
  potatoes
1 teaspoon dried parsley
  flakes
Salt and pepper

1. Start heating oven to 375°F.
2. In large ovenproof skillet or small Dutch oven, in butter, sauté meat cubes, onion, green pepper, and celery until onion is lightly browned.
3. Mix flour with a bit of milk to form a smooth paste; then add remaining milk; add flour-milk mixture to skillet. Cook, stirring constantly, until thickened. Stir in diced potatoes and parsley flakes; reheat to simmer.
4. Bake, uncovered, 40 to 50 minutes, or until potatoes are tender and surface lightly browned. When done, taste sauce and add salt and pepper as desired. Makes 6 servings. (305 *calories per serving*)

CHICKEN-MUSHROOM SOUFFLÉ

1 cup skim milk or
  reliquefied nonfat dry
  milk
¼ cup regular all-purpose
  flour
½ cup sliced fresh mush-
  rooms, or 1 3- or 4-
  ounce can mushroom
  stems and pieces,
  drained

2 tablespoons butter or
  margarine
1 cup finely-diced, cooked
  chicken
½ teaspoon celery salt
½ teaspoon salt
4 eggs, separated

1. Start heating oven to 350°F.
2. In medium saucepan, slowly add milk to flour, stirring constantly to form a smooth paste. Cook, over medium heat, stirring constantly, until mixture simmers and is thick and smooth; remove from heat.
3. Stir in mushrooms, butter, chicken, celery salt, and salt until smooth; stir in egg yolks.
4. In large bowl, beat egg whites until stiff peaks form. Carefully fold chicken mixture into egg whites. Turn into greased 1½-quart casserole.
5. Bake 45 to 55 minutes, or until soufflé is golden-brown on top. Serve immediately. Makes 4 servings. (240 *calories per serving*)

BAKED CHICKEN CASSEROLE

Salt
1 cup elbow macaroni
2 cups skim milk or
  reliquefied nonfat dry
  milk
¼ cup regular all-purpose
  flour
2 chicken-bouillon cubes,
  or 2 envelopes chicken-
  bouillon powder
2 cups diced, cooked
  chicken
½ teaspoon marjoram
Dash pepper

¼ cup snipped parsley
¼ cup chopped onion
1 cup diced celery
3 to 5 fresh mushrooms,
  sliced, or 1 3- or 4-ounce
  can mushroom stems
  and pieces, drained
  (optional)
2 tablespoons chopped
  green pepper
1 tablespoon pimento
  (optional, but a very
  nice addition)
More snipped parsley

About 1 hour before serving:
1. Start heating oven to 350°F.
2. In salted, boiling water, cook macaroni as package label directs; drain.
3. In 2-quart metal or ceramic cookware casserole, slowly add milk to flour, stirring constantly to form a smooth paste. Add bouillon cubes; cook on range top, stirring constantly, until bouillon is dissolved and sauce is thickened and smooth.
4. Stir in cooked macaroni, chicken, marjoram, pepper, ¼ cup snipped parsley, chopped onion, diced celery, mushrooms, chopped green pepper, 2 teaspoons salt, and pimento.
5. Bake, uncovered, 25 to 30 minutes, or until top of casserole is bubbly. Sprinkle generously with more snipped parsley. Makes 5 ample servings. (250 *calories per serving*)

CREAMED TUNA ROCKEFELLER

1 10-ounce package frozen
  chopped spinach, thawed
¼ cup cooked salad
  dressing
5 tablespoons regular all-
  purpose flour
1 teaspoon salt
2 cups skim milk or
  reliquefied nonfat dry
  milk

¼ green pepper, minced
2 tablespoons minced
  onion
1 6½- or 7-ounce can tuna,
  thoroughly drained
½ cup grated Cheddar
  cheese

About 45 minutes before serving:
1. Start heating oven to 350°F.
2. Carefully press all excess moisture from thawed spinach, then divide it equally among 4 greased ovenproof ramekins or individual casserole dishes.
3. In medium saucepan, mix together salad dressing,

flour, and salt to form a smooth paste; slowly stir in milk until smooth; add green pepper and onion. Cook, stirring constantly, until smooth and thick.

4. Divide sauce evenly among ramekins. Break tuna into small pieces; divide among ramekins. Sprinkle cheese evenly on top of tuna.

5. Bake 20 minutes, or until cheese is melted and sauce bubbles. Makes 4 servings. (300 calories per serving)

OYSTERS DIABLE

16 large shucked oysters, or 2 7½-ounce cans oysters	¼ teaspoon prepared or dry mustard
Skim milk or reliquefied nonfat dry milk	2 tablespoons prepared horse-radish
2½ tablespoons regular all-purpose flour	1 teaspoon Worcestershire
¾ teaspoon salt	2 teaspoons lemon juice
⅛ teaspoon pepper	2 cups toasted ½-inch bread squares
¼ teaspoon paprika	¾ cup chopped celery
	Celery leaves

1. Start heating oven to 400°F.
2. Drain oysters, reserving liquid; to liquid add enough milk to measure 2 cups liquid.
3. In saucepan, mix flour, salt, pepper, paprika, and mustard. Gradually add liquid, stirring until smooth. Stir in horse-radish, Worcestershire, and lemon juice. Cook, over low heat, stirring until smooth.
4. In each of 4 12-ounce individual casseroles, arrange layer of bread squares; cover with layers of celery, drained oysters, and sauce. Top with remaining bread squares.
5. Bake 20 to 25 minutes, or until bubbly. Garnish with celery leaves. Makes 4 servings. (225 calories per serving)

CURRIED SHRIMP SOUFFLÉ

1 4½-ounce can shrimp	1 teaspoon curry powder
1 tablespoon butter or margarine	¾ cup milk
1 small onion, sliced	¼ teaspoon salt
1 clove garlic	1 cup cottage cheese
2 tablespoons regular all-purpose flour	3 egg yolks
¼ teaspoon ginger	1 tablespoon snipped parsley
	3 egg whites

1. Start heating oven to 300°F.
2. Drain, rinse well, and devein shrimp; chop coarsely.
3. In hot butter, in saucepan, sauté onion and garlic until soft; remove garlic. Combine flour, ginger, and curry powder; gradually add milk, stirring until smooth; pour over onion; add salt. Cook, over low heat, until thickened.
4. Beat together cottage cheese and egg yolks; gradu-

ally stir in hot mixture. Add shrimp and parsley; remove from heat.

5. Beat egg whites until stiff peaks form; fold shrimp mixture into egg whites. Pour into 4 12-ounce individual casseroles.

6. Bake 40 to 45 minutes, or until silver knife, inserted in center, comes out clean. Serve at once. Makes 4 servings. (225 calories per serving)

TIP-TOP ORANGE PUDDING

½ tablespoon finely-grated orange peel	1 package regular vanilla-pudding-and-pie-filling mix
4 medium oranges, peeled, cut into sections	3 egg whites
2 tablespoons granulated sugar	6 tablespoons granulated sugar
2 cups skim milk or reliquefied nonfat dry milk	Generous dash salt
	½ teaspoon vanilla extract

At least 1 hour before serving:
1. Prepare orange peel. Arrange orange sections in 1½-quart casserole. Press juice from pulp into casserole. Sprinkle orange sections with 2 tablespoons sugar.
2. Start heating oven to 325°F.
3. In medium saucepan, slowly stir milk and orange peel into pudding mix. Cook, stirring constantly, as directed on package label; pour hot pudding over orange sections.
4. In medium bowl, beat egg whites until soft peaks form. Gradually beat in 6 tablespoons sugar, salt, and vanilla; beat until stiff peaks form. Spread meringue over top of pudding, sealing all around edges.
5. Bake 15 minutes, or until peaks of meringue are golden brown.
6. Cool about 30 minutes and serve warm. Makes 8 servings. (155 calories per serving)

GEORGIA DELIGHT

1 1-pound 4-ounce can freestone-peach slices	¼ cup quick-cooking tapioca
¼ teaspoon salt	1 cup boiling water
Generous dash nutmeg	⅓ cup heavy cream, whipped, sweetened
⅛ teaspoon cinnamon	
2 tablespoons lemon juice	

Make day before, or up to 1 hour before serving:
1. Start heating oven to 375°F.
2. In 1½-quart casserole, stir together peaches with their syrup, salt, nutmeg, cinnamon, lemon juice, and tapioca; add boiling water.
3. Bake 30 minutes, or until tapioca is clear, stirring every 10 minutes.
4. Serve warm, or cold, topped with whipped cream. Makes 6 servings. (130 calories per serving)

Index